{Praise}

Licking Flames is like watching Courtney Love sing 'My Way.' At turns funny and biting, Kirk offers a sharp exploration into what it means to be a bold woman in a world built by and for men ~ Ariel Gore, author of *The End of Eve*

Sexy, raw, at times funny, and so so real. I read the whole thing in one sitting, and by the end, I felt like I'd hung out with my best friend. ~ Kerry Cohen, author of *loose girl: a memoir of promiscuity*

Kirk's essays are delicious and satisfying, like slipping away from a stuffy party to drink wine and eat pancakes, or spilling your biggest secret to the one friend who will truly appreciate it. Bold, funny, and unapologetically real. ~ Megan Kruse, author of *Call Me Home*

All of the essays were damn good and some were brilliant. Kirk has a very muscular style of writing. ~ Milo Samardzija, author of *Wassermann Gardens*

When you read something that makes you laugh, cry and snort tea all over your keyboard—sometimes in the same sentence—then you've found an author you can really get into. One day I hope to meet Diana Kirk in person, preferably at a bar where I can buy her a drink, get up to some shenanigans and talk the night away. ~ Kate Pearce, *NY Times* and *USA Today* bestselling author

Diana Kirk peels herself like an onion, revealing a vast array of incarnations from horny bumbling teen to mortuary receptionist; house-flipping mama to humbled international volunteer. ~ Ayun Halliday, author of *No Touch Monkey*

Kirk's writing and a tab of acid could change the minds of many young people today. ~ Rick Peck, founder of The Universal Church of the Good Monkey

Licking Flames is a vivid, funny, well-composed collection. I strongly identify with her tales of mothering and travel; juggling family and business. She writes with a powerful authentic voice, entertaining while raising important questions. ~ Anna Yarrow, artist-in-residence at El Zaguán, Santa Fe

This book is a like a breath of fresh air...in a smoke filled bar. Diana's sarcastic sense of humor will have you laughing until your stomach cramps. Her "no holds barred" style of storytelling makes you feel like you are right there on her crazy adventures and leaves you wanting more. The situations could happen to any of us, which is what makes it even more relatable. I give this book two ass-cheeks up (or five stars, whichever you prefer). ~ Amy Zellmer, author of *Life With a Traumatic Brain Injury: Finding the Road Back to Normal*

Diana Kirk asks unladylike questions about everything. She speculates on the motivations and grisly details behind our official narratives. The vignettes in *Licking Flames* reveal a spirit born to defy stereotype: Kirk's narrator cannot be content as a mother or a businesswoman; she propels herself into new encounters with a primal appetite. Kirk serves as a humane and comic guide, probing the nature of her lovers and chance encounters in such an intimate way that I find myself wanting to know where these characters are now. ~ Jennifer Robin, author of *Death Confetti*

Licking Flames

Tales

of a

Half-Assed

Hussy

Licking Flames

Tales

of a

Half-Assed

Hussy

DIANA KIRK

Go Lick Some Flames

Diana

Black Bomb Books
Asheville, NC
www.BlackBombBooks.com
blackbombbooks@gmail.com

Copyright © 2016 Diana Kirk
ISBN 978-0-692-73009-6
First Edition, December 2016
Cover image by Tim Lukeman

For Steve,

who keeps the soap in my box

{Foreword}

This book is a memoir. Ish.

So, it's all totally true. Kinda.

Except for the parts that aren't.

{Contents}

{1}

Viking Plunder

He stands on a stage with a microphone while a shade of mauve lights cover his black goth fanfic writer-superhero costume. Black T-shirt, black hoodie under a black leather vest with a black kilt above black combat boots that frame his strawberry blonde chest-length tresses I know smell like Axe. Forest flavor. I bet he's fertile like testosterone and clean sweat with just a hint of jiz and smegma mixed over hot breaths in a backseat.

"Alta's pheromones trigger Quattra's arousal."

The open mic host raised the microphone to reach all six foot two inches of his muscled body when he came onstage. Introduced as the newest, hottest writer in this subgenre of subgenres of who cares. Look at his fucking hair! Ginger. And a little ginger PT on his chin. Hell...yes.

An ambulance passes outside, its lights filtering in through the bar windows only half-covered in heavy red velvet drapery. He continues his latest published fanfic piece while a tick tock sounds from a heater mounted above my head.

"She would always be his painted milky way and he would plunge happily into her abyss under any incarnation."

Tick tock. His chin moves up and down exhaling his sci fi soft porn in a voice fitting my attentions. It's deep. Confident. Up and down his breath goes on about futures without celestial strolls between globules of plasma floating overly sexed-up central nervous systems.

His forearm teases an all red Celtic knot under his sweatshirt sleeve. He's a Viking. A Blackguard. I bet he has a sword over his bed. And a shield. Something he carved himself at an SCA convention where they pretend fight for their lady's hand. I start designing my lady's dress. It would be blue with a tight chest. Lots of cleavage. I'd wear my hair down. He likes long hair. He flicks his back behind his shoulder.

"Will Alta find his relief in coupling?" He's louder now over the neighboring theater's punk band blaring out the Sex Pistols 'God Save the Queen.' "Will Quattra benefit from her mating ritual? Will completion even be possible amongst their current forms?"

He lifts weights. He has to. You don't get chest muscles that poke out of a T-shirt, a hoodie, and a leather vest without barbells and grilled chickens breasts. He can cook. Now I've decided he can cook. Steak. Red meat with a salad. He grills it on an outside barbecue near his apartment door. Cow hearts, too. Because he's a Viking.

"Quattra separates her particles before Alta mounts her."

He pauses and looks out at the audience. It's his dramatic pause. I still have no idea what his story is about but I'm sitting on a the edge of my barstool in front of the lit mirrored wall of liquor bottles—sucking in my breath, pushing out my tits, willing his eyes to mine. Please look deeply into my eyes, Mr. Viking boy.

"Quattra's liquid internals surround Alta's atoms as they begin a moving mass of nuclear..."

I've decided I'll climb him like a tree. Like a coconut tree where you wrap your legs around the trunk and pull yourself up higher and higher until his puffy bottom lip hits the inside of my thigh. He's been climbed before. He'd know what to do. Vikings would know how to plunder. I want...to be plundered...by his mouth.

"Quattra and Alta complete. She still oozing onto what once was a cement and rebar office. He collecting his lost atoms that would soon be harvested for another incarnation. And Quattra would have to spend a millennia finding his pheromones ...again."

I clap. He steps away from the mic with a hair toss while the crowded room of supporters whistle and snap their brotherly love. Viking boy heads to the bar, a few friends stopping to shake his hand and back slap his leather vest. I take a deep breath and push my chair to the side, making a spot open for his huge shoulders at the bar.

He takes it with a nod and a shy smile.

Oh dear, he's a shy Viking. And he does smell like Axe. Forest flavor.

Now I want his Viking babies. I want ten of them. With his what, blue eyes? I smile back, lean over to his ear and say, "Well done."

"Thanks," he mumbles towards the bar.

He doesn't see it yet. Me in my blue dress with the tight corset. Our beautiful Icelandic babies he lets hang on his monstrous biceps. I'll bake Scandinavian something-or-others on a Sunday afternoon while he teaches them how to build a boat using his bare hands and some tool you make during a vision quest.

Before I lean over to tell him our granddaughter will remind him of his mother, my phone rings Adele's "Hello" in my purse. Viking boy turns towards the sultry voice in amongst the punk band's current lyric being screamed next door.

"Excuse me," I mumble to myself and turn away as I reach inside my bag.

"Hello?

"I told you I was going out tonight.

"Why can't you put them to bed?

"Give him his blankie and leave the hall light on.

"Did you check for a fever?

"Fine, I'll come home now.

"No, it's fine.

"Really, I'm fine."

{2}

Fuckery Economics

My mom is a hustler. As a kid, I watched her negotiate for ride shares and babysitting. She traded houses for boats, yard work for English lessons. I watched her make deals. She is an opportunist and has honed her skills to lead an intriguing life. This week she's flying an airplane to Baja, and next week she's organizing biking groups for women over seventy. At her core, the very core of all this hustling, is curiosity. She wants to try new things, sometimes out of her comfort zone. She taught me along the way that everyone has something interesting they do or say, and maybe we should be interested, too.

Me, I'm not a very deep person. Like, I don't think about things metaphysically or cosmically. I have a short attention span like a Neanderthal...food, sex, hunt; I read junk books sometimes; I eat junk food sometimes; I do dumb things, and I don't really feel bad about any of it. The junk and the dumb are interesting in the moment. I suppose I should worry, think deeper. Maybe I have an internal shortage of giving-a-fucks. If I want to take a two-hour bath in the afternoon and eat Andes mints while my kids watch TV, I just do it. I've always done exactly what I want. My way.

I've tried on the serious "I give a fuck" lifestyles, for sure. I tried on vegetarian, granola, clearcutting protestor in the nineties. I was an REI name-dropping world tramper and an attachment parenting, home-birthing, double-extended nursing mama who then became a mini-muffin, juice-box soccer mom. I did the Wednesday soup-canning exchange club and the homemade-laundry-soap-while-drinking-wine women's group. (That last one was fun.)

That's kind of the basis of all of my choices. They were fun at the time. Deep down, I wasn't crying about the spotted owl losing its habitat from clear-cuts; I just liked camping in the redwoods with hot hippie men. I was a fraud. I'm still a fraud.

I suppose I'm in a new phase of giving-a-fuck right now, and I don't even know it. It doesn't have a name yet. That's kind of exciting to me. But it will have a name, and the moment I figure it out, then I'll probably move onto something else fad-ishly new, again. I'm assuming it will entail either dyeing my graying hair or making Mexican border runs for cheap dental care. I think it'll be fun because I'll be surrounded, like I always have been, with passionate people who for now, think differently than I do.

Which is the key for this life of mine, for sure. Find interesting people to surround yourself with. People who collect Kewpie dolls, study lithography, work as whores. I really don't enjoy all like-minded groups of folks. Never have. It's why I leave every group eventually. The people start to sound the same; they talk the same. Once I figure out how they talk, I move on. I can feel my brain grow whenever I'm in a situation that is completely foreign to me.

Good or bad.

Like when I'm with my cousin and her business friends whom I've dubbed the Rieslings. Being with them, well, it's like trying to eat cracked crab at Tavern on the Green. I'm all tip-toeing around their white wine puff-pastry world, trying my hardest not to blurt out a story about the time I watched two grizzlies fight over a dead moose calf in Alaska. My mind flips through covers I've seen at the grocery store, hoping something will jog a conversation out of me about the newest açai berry nostril cleanser. I want them to talk about Paleo Crossfit, I want to hear about the fabulous new hair conditioner their stylist told them about so I can buy some at three o'clock, wash my hair by three-fifteen and by four o'clock drop the same info on a new unsuspecting victim at the grocery store.

"Yeah, it's made with rabbit urine which is super high in magnesium from all the folic acid they eat, so it really softens your hair. Just feel it."

I want to be one of them for a two-hour lunch, these women I don't belong with. Except they know I'm a fraud. Their tight-lipped smiles are only seconds away from turning on me and saying, all Regina George, "Weren't you the one who lived in a school bus?"

I am. I am that woman who lived with her family for three years in a school bus in Mexico and Canada. Because that was what I was really into back then. But I'm also a lot of other women. I'm that woman who worked in law firms, mortuaries, the federal government, the state, for camps, for farms in India and Africa, bird-rescue organizations, schools, non-profits, for-profits, LLCs and S corps. I'm more than any box you get from Amazon. But I don't tell that part. I don't say it out loud because, um, that would be awkward.

I just smile my best crooked smile.

"Yes, we did live in a bus. Drove all over North America. I wanted to show my kids there was more to life than the American dream."

I mean, that's what they want to hear, right? It's fun for a little while to listen to strappy sandal conversations while sipping on a light pear-flavored Riesling from the Klickitat Valley. I enjoy it; I enjoy visiting these worlds that really, I don't belong in.

Good or bad.

So that's what I think about in the bathtub, while eating those chocolate mints and pausing from those trashy books. I don't think about what I probably should think about, like the state of everything everywhere. Ever. And I don't think about the future of our planet or whether my family has eaten enough vegetables this week. I just think about learning fun shit or taking a trip to Croatia, maybe building a container house in Baja, eating Lebanese takeout, how much solar panels cost, who invented underwear?

{3}

Thriller

The full fifteen-minute version of *Thriller* by Michael Jackson blared over the loudspeakers while I couple-skated under a turning disco ball. It was a hot Saturday night at Sunrise Roller Rink, and my sweaty hand was being held by that of Jonathan Martin. The Jonathan Martin. The very guy with black-lashed eyes who'd been driving me into tornado twists of unrequited teenage lust for a solid year.

"So, you wanna skate?" I asked, hoping to sound casual while I tried to catch my breath from winning first prize at speed skate. I avoided his eyes while I stared at the tiniest of beginner whiskers on his chin. My nerves had threatened an accidental lip spittle or at a minimum, a dumb compliment about his rental skates.

"Right now, you wanna skate right now?" He avoided my eyes but stared at my new skin-tight Wham! T-shirt. Yes! He'd noticed. My Mom had almost killed me when I'd taken scissors to it earlier that afternoon to reshape the arms and cut some slits across the stomach.

"So much better," I'd said in front of her while she pretended to pull her hair out.

"Uh yeah, Jonathan, duh," I rolled my eyes. "Come on, you promised you'd skate with me tonight. Let's go." I yanked on his arm until he pushed across the carpeted floors, and we hit the dark rink, hand in hand.

Jonathan was probably too cool to couples-skate, I knew that. He never really did stuff. He observed. The first time I saw him at the Mine Shaft, I was going through a brief but very colorful Madonna stage. With my hair tied back in ripped-up fabric and a polka-dotted mini-skirt, swiveling to the beats, I would sing, "You may be my lucky star," and point my bangled arm toward him from the dance floor. The stage lights blinding me just enough to be so bold.

I knew where he stood. He liked to lean against the wall with his pink Polo button-down and crisp white jeans, hiding in the dark, away from the lights. He knew everything going on around him. Fully aware of Sperry Topsiders and Jordache jeans, real Ray Bans versus fake.

His family was wealthy, like own-an-airplane wealthy. Jonathan Martin Sr. worked as a designer for JC Penney, and his mother was a retired model, which explained his crystal blue eyes and commercial clear skin.

He drove a jacked up yellow Nova he told me meant "star" in some other language. He'd lived in Italy, so he knew stuff like that. I filed it away in my portfolio of perfect Jonathanisms that I would refer to when I listened to the *Pretty in Pink* soundtrack for hours, staring at photos I I'd badgered him into giving me.

"Oh Jonathan," I mooned out loud while New Order tugged at my angst-ridden chest.

It's never enough until your heart stops beating
The deeper you get, the sweeter the pain.

I listened over and over again, writing Mrs. Jonathan Martin on my Algebra Pee-Chee folder, for the gazillionth time. He was my crack before my lungs ever tried a first cigarette.

"Mom, I think I need to go to rehab. I've got a Jonathan problem."

She listened patiently as she changed out of her teacher uniform, a rayon dress with matching earrings, hose and one inch heels. "Honey, we all had a Jonathan problem at your age. If you didn't, you actually would have a problem. Just remember, you are the queen of your own castle..."

"Yes, Mom, I know, I know, and I am the only one to enter."

The addiction was most acute on Saturday nights when I saw his newest Amber or Jennifer and their 36Cs—hair pulled to the side, falling loosely around their faces and yet in perfect symmetry. I danced myself sweaty and dreamed that my hand would get caught in their giant white hoops, ripping their ears apart. But they never got close enough with their upturned noses and rolling eyes. They literally never moved except to take a drink.

He smiled at me, sometimes, I swear it. If our eyes met during the night. Usually, when I did something stupid like pinch my friend's butt or trip in my roman sandals. A small curl on his perfect lips would appear, quick. It was the little things that kept my addiction going. I knew he noticed me, watched me. Maybe he even liked me better than those perfect blue-mascaraed Ambers and Jennifers.

Despite our "moments," I'd always end the night sobbing in my room blaring Culture Club while my mother rubbed my back.

"There are always other fish in the ocean Diana. Jonathan isn't the only boy out there."

Ugh, she just didn't understand!

She'd never met my Jonathan. I mean girls would stare at him when he walked into a club. Stare, jaws-dropped staring, while he sauntered across the dance floor to find his wall. Then he'd throw me a quick glance up onstage where I would be pulling my latest Bananarama dance moves. All those girls watching him and he looked at me. Me! Then the strobelights and the ecstasy of his glance would spin me into a *Tiger Beat* high, thus continuing to feed the bittersweet addiction. Nobody understood what we had. I knew him. We had a thing. No Amber or Jennifer or Mom was gonna understand the way we connected.

"Hey Jonathan, how you doing tonight?"

"Good."

"How's your car driving?"

"Good. I got an oil change."

"Really, that's cool. Drive better now?"

"Um, no. It always drives good."

"Well, I mean, yeah, cool."

They didn't understand those kinds of chats. I mean, he actually talked to me! Rarely did he talk to other people. Not even his girlfriends. But I knew his car meant the world to him. He told me one day he'd even give me a ride. It never worked out though, 'cause Mom always picked me up from the teen clubs in our giant station wagon.

Tonight though, right now, he was holding my hand as we circled the skating rink during minute five of *Thriller*. His Ralph Lauren had hit my nostrils long ago and was causing some serious butterflies deep inside my castle to start clawing out of their cocoons. Good god, how was I supposed to get over how soft his hands were and how magnificent his profile looked, turn after turn around the rink?

On minute eight of *Thriller*, other couples started to zombie-arm each other, laughing while they mimicked the MTV dance moves. I giggled and felt my own shoulders bob up and down a few times. Not Jonathan though. His slicked-back hair didn't move in the wind, and his face was etched in place, chiseled in stone.

My shoulder couldn't stop itself anymore despite my efforts. More bobbing and then my head maybe did a little stiff circle move to the beat of the music. It was happening. My zombie body was awakening.

Laughing at myself, I looked over at him—his turquoise Polo shirt with its stiff upturned collar and not a bead of sweat anywhere to be seen. Perfect like a Greek statue. I mean, if statues could look annoyed at zombie wannabes while roller-skating.

People started to chase each other, screaming in mock fear. I squealed when a boy grabbed my waist and bared his teeth like a hungry brain eater. Every part of my body wanted to hiss back and start chasing him around the rink.

I glanced down at Jonathan's hand holding mine. We'd never held hands before. He had manicured fingernails and flawless skin. But my fingers were twitching, the music taking effect, challenging my body to give in.

So I gave his hand a last squeeze and smiled at him right before I let go. I...let...go.

In a flash, I went after a woman skating next to me, grabbed at her shoulders while she shrieked and pretended to eat her. Everyone was chasing one another, laughing while the music blared. People standing next to the rink joined in, shooting imaginary guns at us zombies. Everyone had become a giant B-rated movie, even the refs and DJ joined in.

Jonathan got lost in the mayhem, but I didn't bother to look for him because I knew him better than anyone. This wasn't Jonathan's thing. He was meant for something else. People like Jonathan never became zombies.

{4}

Pink Wrestle-Mania

Mike T. and his giant cock were in my art class, freshman year, third period. He'd agreed to help me shed my virgin stigma as we were making silk-screened Van Halen T-shirts.

"I just want it gone. I don't care how. I'm so tired of thinking about it."

"I'll do it," he said. "I'll pop that cherry of yours."

We were to meet at midnight at the park near my house. I shaved and picked out my best pink undies with matching bra and sprayed Love's Baby Soft on my neck. Mike may have been a sure thing, but his reputation as a star wrestler required some effort on my part. I felt lucky he'd even offered.

At eleven thirty p.m., I started wavering. About my ponytail, my mint gum, my pink sweats. Maybe I'd be sexier if I didn't wear undies?

"Enough," I finally told myself in my dresser mirror before climbing out my bedroom window.

The park was empty and semi-dark at the end of my cul de sac with one simple streetlight at the sidewalk. I could see Mike clearly. He leaned against the slide, hands shoved deep in his pockets. He'd wisely chosen a tank top. My late night hormones focused on his cut arms and his fresh shower smell.

"Hey," I mumbled, kicking bark chips around my flip flops.

I heard his deep breath coming toward me and then his tongue was down my throat, and he was pushing me back against the cold metal monkey bars. I'd thought there would be some small talk, but instead there were just hands.

He was a good kisser. Well, an aggressive kisser. He was "experienced," I reminded myself. My sweatpants were already getting pushed to the ground, my shirt getting pulled up. I was sure I wanted to do this, but I was beginning to question his speed.

"Hey, stop," I said, pushing him back and looking up into his disappointed eyes. "I mean don't stop, I mean just slow down for a second, okay?"

He looked at me, starving. But he stopped.

On my third deep breath, I kissed him this time. A gentle brush of my lips against his. I took it slow. I bravely ran my hand down into his shorts where I found his giant bulge. It wasn't my first time touching one or my second. I knew just enough to understand his was quite possibly the largest cock I would ever touch. My sexual instincts began to yell, "There's no way that shlong will fit inside me!"

The sheer size of it was more than could fit in my hand. I couldn't reach around it inside his shorts. I couldn't remember anything I'd learned in eighth grade summer camp. My mind was blank from fear.

What had Cosmo told me to do? Was I supposed to squeeze it?

Mike's tongue was beginning to overpower my mouth again, suffocating me. I gasped for breath while his stubbly sophomoric face scratched against mine, his fingers pinching my nipples too hard, his body pushing my hand more and more against his giant penis.

Everything sped up. Too fast. The grabbing and squeezing and now his hand was in my pink panties, his finger shoving inside me, when it all just stopped.

His arm muscles went rigid under my hand. His breath stopped. I just sat there squeezing his dick, frozen in place. Scared to move.

And that's when I noticed. My hand down his pants was covered in goo.

The shamed expression when he pulled away from me said it all. It was over. I felt like somebody had dumped a bucket of cold water on my head.

"Oh my god," I said, searching for an invisible towel to wipe my hand on. Cosmo didn't tell me what to do now. What does a person say when this happens. "I'm sorry?"

My sweats were around my ankles, my shirt around my shoulders and a shot of jiz dangled on my fingers a block from my house where my parents slept. It was a school night.

Dear God, it's me Diana. What do I do now?

Mike's giant cock shriveled like a slug inside his underwear. He kept staring at the ground. His giant arm muscles twitching. The awkwardness choking both of us. My virginity...still intact.

{5}

Nancy

I had a short-lived punk rock stage in high school. It mainly had to do with my newly minted step-brother who was going through his own short-lived skinhead stage and with my own personal attraction to extremism. Our newly conjoined parents wanted their quiet canoodling time together without their "punk" daughter and "skinhead" son, so they'd hand us the keys to the Trans Am and twenty bucks for a night out.

My step-brother was older, so he would drive me around to downtown clubs where Black Flag, Agent Orange, and the Circle Jerks might be playing. He'd disappear with the other Doc Martin fake Brit boys from our Northern California suburban 'hood while I'd dance inside under strobe lights. It was at a show that I first saw Henry Rollins and fell in lust, and also the first time I'd been somewhere that turned into a crime scene. While rolling around through a mosh pit, someone had taken an ice pick to the heart. The crowd broke out running, and I ended up all alone on the street surrounded by broken glass, cops, and no Trans Am and no step-brother.

I really didn't love the music. I loved Henry Rollins. I didn't love the mosh pit either, but I loved dancing with a tiny bottle of Rush in my pocket. I was pretty vain about my hair and wouldn't cut it into a mohawk or dye it blue, but I did cut it into a flat top because a bi-level feathered doo did not scream hardcore. And I wanted hardcore. I wanted broken bottles and angsty teenagers. I wanted to see the frayed ends where people wore their emotions. Where I wore mine.

And I was a moth, flittering around the edges of whatever might possibly kinda maybe hurt me.

It was during this extremely short-lived stage that I read a book written by Deborah Spungen called *And I Don't Want to Live this Life*. The book is about Deborah's daughter, Nancy Spungen. She was married to Sid Vicious, bassist for the Sex Pistols. Sid famously stabbed his wife Nancy in the Chelsea Hotel in 1978 where she bled to death a few months later before he overdosed to join her.

Their love story is sadly not unique but did come before Kurt and Courtney and Amy and Blake. Even fucked-up people can have a love story, right? I mean Nancy was a sex worker in London and Sid was a bad boy musician. He introduced her to the rock'n'roll life, and she introduced him to heroin. One night, exhausted from months of shooting, Nancy begged Sid to end her life. At twenty years old. It screams of Romeo and Juliet.

Difficult right out of the womb, Nancy's parents let her go at a young age when they discovered they could not control anything about her— from the drugs, to the sex, or the abuse she inflicted upon them. At thirteen. Her need for attention was insatiable. At sixteen, she was sent to college. But nothing could satisfy Nancy's extremism. They decided before Tough Love was even a thing, to let her do whatever it was she needed to do. Something in me related to something in her. Her need to flee, her need to do it her way. Moth to flame.

I became obsessed. She was the first real person I'd ever heard of who worked in the sex industry by choice. At that point in my life, at fifteen, I thought all sex workers were being pimped out by men who beat them and took their money. Nancy was a fresh, dark, post-Judy Blume twist in the confusing story of sex and women who swirled through my hormone-thick body. Nancy was a dominatrix in London, living a somewhat normal life in an apartment with tea and toast in leather G-strings. Even her mother said she seemed happier working there.

In 1986 when I was sixteen, the movie *Sid and Nancy* came out starring Gary Oldman and Chloe Webb—with a small cameo by Courtney Love. As a sometimes-sad teenager, I fell in love with their image on the big screen. They were my Catherine and Heathcliff, my fucked-up *Sixteen Candles*. Morose, dark, romantic in their own way. Painful, brutal, disturbingly morbid. It was a voyeuristic love snapshot into people's truth between the sheets, between their words, and between their eyes. It felt more real to me than most of my real life.

Maybe it was the timing. Maybe I was a lovesick teenager looking for a few answers to life. But somehow, at sixteen, I learned this from the book. We have, within our grasp, the choice of free will. That despite being surrounded by people, media, and literature yelling at me, attempting to shame me into submission, into conformity, projecting happiness as a goal...that I could choose to live with my eyes wide open instead. Nancy Spungen wouldn't let anyone tell her how to live or even to die.

And I've been following suit, in my own much more conservative way, ever since.

{6}

After

Cocaine and I were instantly the bestest of friends. Stuffed up my nose, she felt like a Calvin Klein dress on Oscars night. I could do no wrong. I was the wittiest, funniest, most interesting person sitting on the black leather couch at a Sacramento drug dealer's three-bedroom, one-bath seventies ranch-style suburban house. And if I stayed as funny as I could, there would be more coke put on a mirror by the older men who came and went all night to the backroom, where they purchased eight-balls from my best friend's much much older and occasionally violent boyfriend.

Of course, I eventually procured my own violent boyfriend. His name was Seth. He had bamboozled my heart at seventeen with his blue eyes and video game conspiracy theories.

"No, you see the Man watches how we play Tron and then profiles us using a corneal traction to guarantee we don't work for the Russians."

We met soon after he had partially reformed, following the year he lived in a boys home, which was after a rehab program for huffing paint. I saw nothing but good looks and a large IQ.

We set up house in an apartment, and I made lasagnas from scratch. We had people over for lines of coke and midnight swims in our apartment pool: Beth from work and her twenty-five-year-old boyfriend Mark who drove a black 280ZX; Mark's roommate David, who constantly licked his lips; and Brian, an up-and-coming stand up comedian who, for some reason, always seemed to keep an eye on me. These friends also told me Seth cheated with other girls at concerts and parties, but I never believed it. They were just jealous because Seth had a girlfriend who made lasagna.

After time and repetition, things changed. Seth grew distant as I started community college classes. Then I smelled paint on his breath one afternoon and he began disappearing for days on end. Then he punched me in the face in our living room when I asked where he'd been. Punched hard. That day I moved home to Mom and my stepdad, but yet I still couldn't let go of Seth. I loved him. I needed to check and make sure he was eating. Despite every person's warning, I still went and tracked him down a few weeks later. If it wasn't for that one night at his mother's house—where he had been huffing paint for days, and where I found him naked and paranoid on the kitchen floor—he probably wouldn't have rearranged my cheekbones with his fist while proving his fucked-up manhood between my thighs. I probably wouldn't have spent a year hiding in my parent's house after, and I would have never ever needed sweet Jon or the Church of Jesus Christ of Latter Day Saints.

The church part started with Marnie. We became friends while she trained me to become a replacement receptionist in a slow office with hours of chit-chat time in between. She laughed a lot. Like at everything. Giggling about boys and puppies and the Kentucky Fried Chicken's new Chicken Littles we obsessively ate. She could also be serious with tears and a frown between her eyes when I told her stories about the boys I'd already lost. Not Seth. I didn't talk about Seth to anyone.

Marnie had two emotions, but the happy one was contagious. I wanted to make her laugh and smile. It gave me a high I hadn't felt in so long. I'd broken it off with everyone in my life after that night with Seth. Everyone who did things I couldn't be around anymore. Like cocaine and fucking.

Marnie wrote in a journal with a black leather cover. It said Latter Days Saints on the spine, and she bought me one as well. Not to convert me but because I had professed a liking to the large pages with the crisp lines going across. We stayed friends past her last day at the office. She moved onto a bank, and I stayed with my journal answering the phones. Writing, daily. Pages and pages of writing. More words than I had spoken in a year.

"Hey, you said you played volleyball in high school. I go to this thing on Thursday nights where they play pick-up. You wanna come?"

It sounded fun. I felt ready to enter the world of socializing again. She seemed easy to be friends with which is what I needed more than therapy or a prescription. My days and nights had been reduced to work, a few college classes, and watching TV with my parents after barbecued chicken and salad dinners. I had nothing to lose at that point. We made plans for a Thursday.

Now when Marnie had said a pick-up game, I'd pictured a few

friends bouncing a ball back and forth over a sagging net. I had not pictured a gym, attached to a church with 200 teenagers whipping balls around in well-formed, rotating teams. I was instantly intimidated by this new world, new people, new ideas. I had never been around this many Mormons.

I became a regular. I looked forward to it every week. With music blaring overhead, I'd play on the middle court, wait my turn, and pull my signature high school serve that would pull out five or six points per rotation. It felt comfortable. It felt competitive but not in that outsmarting another cokehead kind of way. It felt simpler. Nobody in the room knew me. Nobody knew about my past. Nobody really saw me at all, and I was okay with that. I didn't want to be noticed.

Other people came just for the volleyball and had no relationship to the church. Most, though, were ring-wearing LDS churchgoers with a future mission planned. They didn't swear or talk about getting fucked up on Friday nights. After a few weeks, I started getting invited to other pickup games around town. Behind churches I'd never noticed before. Invariably, someone's older brother or sister had a key to a swimming pool owned by the church—that shockingly entrusted the keys to a teenager—and we'd go swimming fully clothed.

But I did notice people. I noticed the boys. These were corn-fed virgins. Their religious innocence was so foreign. After years of hanging out with people on the edge, I was suddenly learning another language. There were no sexual undertones to conversations. No innuendos or double entendres.

"Hey, I notice you always wear red. It's my favorite color."

"Oh really. You know what they say about girls who wear red?"

"They like Christmas?"

The boys asked me what church I went to, what my last name was. Nobody seemed to care I wasn't a "member." These were still young people just trying to have fun within the rules of their society. They were polite. They were kind and inclusive. We danced to loud music, we did doughnuts in parking lots in stick-shift cars. Only without beer bongs. We played games late in neighborhood parks and snuck people into drive-in movies where no sex was had in backseats. It was sweet. Like middle school with part-time jobs and driver's licenses.

I had spent a solid year in monotony *after*. Routine became my therapy. Work, school, home. Zero time seeking out anything with feels. Friends were non-existent. My family, calm and quiet. I had done nothing and been nothing for a whole year with few emotions. I had seen violence and rage before and it had turned on me. I swore I would not become a lifelong victim of that one night, and the innocent safe bubble of these Mormons was reminding me exactly what it was to have a life. To be young and free and safe. To be a young adult on my own. No pressure from anyone. I needed to feel free again until I could put one foot back into that meadow.

And on a warm summer evening, when a group of us were looking for Mormon trouble, you know, like throwing fireworks off bridges, a car pulled up and a very cute guy jumped out of the back. Dark. Dark skin, dark hair, dark eyes, full lips. Nothing about him said, "I'm a member of the Church of Jesus Christ of Latter Day Saints." He dressed like a surfer, talked like a stoner, and admired my tits as if from experience. My libido yelled "Hello, big boy." My *after* may have just arrived.

"Hey, I heard you play volleyball?"

"I do, I heard you windsurf?"

"I do."

His smile was gorgeous. Perfect white teeth up against summer-tanned skin. The fact he wasn't very smart kinda helped. I wasn't seeking any IQ dance-athons. My earlier life choices had now humbled me right into community college, and I really didn't want to be around Nietzsche or Dostoevsky buffs. He just wanted to surf and bike and hike and camp and do all the stuffs I needed to do to remember life. And he made me laugh while we did it. He tickled but never held my hand. He touched my hair but never kissed my neck. He watched me through a crowd but never walked over. It was there. All *Sixteen Candles* soundtrack. But I could see it behind his long lashes, his virginity was going to be a problem.

And so one night he stopped by my house and asked if we could go for a walk. It was in an abandoned building near our house under a full moon that he leaned down while chomping on gum and gave me an oh so sloppy kiss. He wasn't very experienced. At anything. So we fondled. FOREVER. We were nineteen. It seemed silly to think that we would just hold hands until what, he returned from a mission? Every part of my body wanted to get naked with this gorgeous thing that smelled good and felt good and tasted good. He was clean. And safe. I told him my ex-boyfriend was a huffer. He'd never heard of it before, let alone free-basing coke. He was springtime. Bambi with his big brown eyes. I just wanted to curl up in his lap for the rest of my life and watch reruns while licking his chest.

I've never had church guilt. I've never felt it. I don't even understand it now as I write these words. I didn't try to understand it with Jon. I one hundred percent seduced him on my friend's kitchen floor after three solid months of dry humping him in his backseat. It was a sloppy fuck that happened so fast neither one of us thought for one single second about what we were doing. A part of my brain expected it to hurt and when it didn't, I just got carried away with the me part of it all. Jon and the church, yeah, I felt zero remorse. He'd just broken all the Mormon rules, and I was just happy to be back in the saddle.

Jon didn't seem to care about his Mormon-ism. We took to sex like a Kama Sutra guidebook. He was willing. He was innocent, and I was in charge. I needed to be in charge. I needed to drive this entire relationship or I was never going to have a chance of an *after*.

We dated. We double-dated and did what I thought normal couples do. You laugh with friends, you hold hands, you make out, you have bad breath morning sex. You have dinner parties. You shop for Christmas gifts. For nine months, we had fun. We did the movie montage section of life. I had somehow managed to become...a happy normal teenager.

Until I got a phone call one day from the local bishop at the Mormon center.

"Diana, we'd like you to come in. There's something we need to speak about."

I really had no idea what the subject matter would be. I wasn't a Mormon and despite a few people's efforts here and there, I wasn't going to become a Mormon.

The Bishop with his dark suit and red power tie, thought he had a chance. "The Church needs women like you. It would strengthen us to have more female leaders." He was kind in a used car salesman way, sitting on the edge of his desk in his office and trying to come off casual.

"I really brought you in here to talk about Jon. You know he's going on a mission, don't you?"

"Yes, he's mentioned it."

"Well, the Church expects young men to act accordingly so that when they leave for their mission, they have a pure heart and soul."

Pure. That word hung in the room.

"What is it you're trying to say?" I'd spoken with him before at the volleyball games on Thursday nights. He seemed okay with my lack of religion, but, um, this word *pure* had just come up.

"Well, it's just become obvious to some that maybe Jon isn't making the best choices right now."

Hold up. What did he just say to me? Did this man of god just bring up my sex life in a church office? "You mean because Jon is dating me?"

"No, not the dating part. But perhaps what intimacies you two are sharing."

I wanted to cry. When I'm angry, I want to cry. And yell and kick and scream and yell again. No, no, no, no! *You're not going to take this away from me!* I don't really know how I changed physically, but I've seen photos of myself angry. My nostrils flare, and I kick my leg a little. I'm sure my legs were crossed in his office because Mom raised me with manners, but I'm sure my leg was kicking.

"Are you trying to say that this is somehow my fault?"

"I'm saying that young men are vulnerable around strong women such as you. They lose their faith."

Yes, he was going to say this was my fault. That I had seduced Jon. I had pressured him with my slutty ways. Which was true. I did. But I didn't force him. Our sex life had been the best part of my year. I felt good with Jon. Safe. Cherished. Sated.

I looked at his awards on the wall. Row after row of "Bishop of the Year." Framed in oak, they hung on dark paneling lit from an overhead green lamp with the little brass hand puller. I stared at the mauve carpet, his laced-up leather, man-shoes, the wooden door into the hallway. I just couldn't look at his face. I would not look at his face. I would never look at his face again.

"It takes two to tango." I wanted to add 'fucker' to the end. I wanted to call him a dragon-breathing piece-of-shit finger-pointing mutha-fucker.

"Are you planning to punish him for this?"

"No, of course not."

"What would you do if the roles were reversed? What would you do if a young Mormon couple were having sex before a mission? What's the church's normal procedure?"

"Usually we like to keep our boys going on missions."

"What would happen to the girl?"

"Well, every case is different."

"Answer the question." I remember saying this with a raised voice. Keeping my anger is check had never been easy for me, but I felt fury over what I believed to be everything good in my life. "You brought me in here to lecture me on my relationship. You owe me enough to tell me what would happen. If I was a Mormon."

"We would probably ask you to leave the church."

"That's what I thought." Excommunicated. He had simultaneously asked me to join the church and threatened to kick me out if I fucked my boyfriend. Who opened doors for me, bought me stupid teddy bears, and always called when he said he would. He was what girls should date, should marry. The nice ones.

Jon didn't act surprised when I told him about the bishop's meeting. "My mom gave me a talking-to as well." The pressure was on. Jon would be nineteen soon. Nineteen was when Mormon boys go on missions. They come back two years later and marry Mormon girls. The church was making their move, and I wasn't going to be a part of it unless I too wanted to wear an LDS ring and spend three hours on Sundays at church. That was never going to happen.

I left for college a month later. Jon came to visit on campus. It was an awkward weekend. The hand holding felt off. The sex was repetitive. Nothing felt right. I was meeting new people again. People from different cities and different countries. I was ready to hit the clubs, frat parties, and over-indulge my way through college like they do in the movies. He wanted to go camping and make love under the stars. I'd never been in love with him. I think he had merely been my *after*.

Sitting on a park bench next to the biology building, we both decided we were holding on too tight to what was. The time had come to move on to new things. He needed to get ready for his mission. I needed to live my own life. Somewhere between Before and After.

I cried that night once he'd left. I said goodbye to what was, both Seth and Jon. Packaged together in some sort of giant life lesson rolled up in cocaine and the Church of Jesus Christ of Latter Day Saints.

{7}

Firehouse Dogs

Rick was Mom's tenant for fifteen years. He was a hot firefighter and Mom kinda crushed on him. Or maybe I did. He had thinning curly hair and was really flirty with her, but in a shy way that involved winking instead of banter. He'd send her bills for supplies when something broke or needed painting, never bothering Mom to come fix it or hire a contractor herself. And they'd bicker over this ancient oak tree in the backyard whenever we'd stop by to pick up rent or drop off paint. Mom wanted to cut it down for safety, but Rick had built a whole seating area under it with a built-in barbecue and lounge chairs, a kiddie pool for his dogs. Rick loved the tree.

One day, Mom got a call from his firehouse at the end of summer. Rick had died. No seriously, he'd died. My mom had never had a tenant die before.

They wanted to send the chief over to talk to her about it. She was obviously shaken up but felt she didn't need someone to come over.

They insisted. "It's protocol. Rick had no family, and we need to discuss some specific issues related to the house."

Somber and in uniform, the chief and two firefighters arrived at the house. Mom wiped her eyes with a tissue when she answered the door, still in her school teacher dress and hose.

They sat her down and explained that Rick had died in her house. We had assumed it was in the line of duty, because that would have made a better story. Instead, they explained that he had a heart attack while packing for a solo trip. When he didn't return to work after two weeks, they sent someone over to check on him. And that's why they needed to see Mom in person.

You see, Rick had died alone in his house with his two dogs. Before a two-week vacation. Him and his dogs. In the house. Rick dead. Dogs alone. Big dogs. Great Dane dogs. Dogs who get hungry. Rick dead. Rick and the dogs. The dogs and Rick. Oh god, what happened to the dogs! Did the dogs eat Rick?!?

We don't know what happened to the dogs. Nobody told us. But Rick did die in the house, and then stuff happened to his body while he waited to be found.

It was horrifying. Horrifying. Obviously. What was also horrifying was the fact that Mom now had to deal with this house. Where the hot firefighter she'd flirted with had died and decomposed on her carpets. How do you even start? Who do you call to clean that up? Can you rent the house again? Should she sell it? Just replace the carpet? Oh god, the dogs and Rick. Did I mention they were Great Danes? And they were missing?

Mom is a practical woman. She doesn't get lost in deep trenches of denial or sadness for very long. But she could not go into the house. At all. She could barely talk about it. For three weeks, she waited then decided to sell the house. She would never be able to go inside it again with any sort of peace.

Late one night a few weeks later, another phone call came from the firehouse. "We need you to come to Rick's house. You're not gonna believe this."

She went. There were camera crews all around the house, lights blazing when she pulled up. I saw it on the eleven o'clock news from my college apartment a hundred miles away. It was the craziest story on the news that night. The enormous oak tree that Rick loved and Mom hated...had fallen on the house. Crushed it. Totaled it. The insurance company called it a full loss. Nothing was saved but the foundation.

Four weeks after Rick's body had been discovered, a slew of tractors and dump trucks arrived to haul away a hundred-year-old oak tree and a three-bedroom, one-bath house with questionable carpeting. They left a twelve-foot hole in the backyard from the oak tree and a cement foundation. Mom built a new house on top. To this day, she still calls it Rick's house then mumbles something incoherent about the poor dogs and poor Rick.

{8}

Death Too

The ad said: "Front desk receptionist at classy establishment. People skills a must." The man I spoke to on the phone hired me before I even arrived for an interview. Which was strange. I'd worked in some law firms and had a semi-perfect lawyerly voice. Calm and confident. He said I would be a greeter and do light clerical in the evenings and weekends. As a biology major, it was a perfect schedule that would allow me to study while working. And it would be quiet because of the dead people.

I did greet people, alive and grieving people arriving to see their loved ones for the last time. At viewings mainly. Those happened the night before a funeral, when only the families and close friends came and sat with their loved ones in a tiny room, whispering stories, hugging, laughing and crying a lot. People skills were a must, because occasionally—when they'd follow me up the stairs and down the carpeted blue hallways to the rooms with their uncles, grandmothers, friends—sometimes it would be the first time they saw their person, and they'd crumple to the floor and wail.

It happened in my first week when a family arrived dressed in green and gold saris and shiny blue satin double-breasted suits. They arrived somber, as expected, the women with swollen eyes and smeared make-up. They followed me up the sweeping bannister to the second floor and turned down a wide hallway with rooms to the left and right decorated in soft mauves and creamy yellows with silk flower arrangements, until we reached the end. The baby room. Inside the robin's egg blue painted room was a tiny white casket sitting on an oak table holding a perfect doll of a child. A full head of black hair, her eyelashes darkened with kohl, her body dressed in white and pink with tiny patent leather shoes. Maybe she was six months old.

I had already been warned by the staff, probably because I was new. My boss had told me to go see the baby before the family arrived. To be better prepared. When I saw her little body lying on the satin-wrapped padding, she just looked asleep. As if she was down for a nap.

When I reached the baby's room with her family, I stood outside the door to allow them to be the first to enter. Instead, they unexpectedly dropped to their knees; the entire group of five dropped to the ground and began to bellow words or sounds that needed no explanation. Pain. Sadness. All I heard and saw. I stood in my red pencil skirt with white pumps and matching cardigan, my poker face on, before I carefully stepped over their flowing saris to retreat back to my desk and my microbiology books.

Sometimes my job would be to remove a bit of rouge from Uncle

Henry's cheeks or clean some fluid out of his ears that would leak from the inside. They were already decaying, and even embalming fluid for the funeral sometimes leaked out and filled their ear cavities or fell on their pillows. It didn't bother me to do these things. Take a napkin and wipe it up. The bodies didn't scare me. I was nice to them. The dead people.

"Good night Mr. Johnson, sleep well. You, too, Catharine, good-looking grandson you've got there, woman."

Sometimes people arrived and they weren't happy. "My mother didn't look like that. She looks like a whore with all that makeup on."

I'd get out a pad of paper and look concerned. "I'll leave a note for the funeral director. See what they can do." They needed to be heard. I tried my best to listen and solve their problems if I could.

I certainly wouldn't tell them that their mother had been painted with something called "orange juice," which was really what gave their skin any color at all. Darryl, one of the funeral directors, had allowed me to watch him prep a body from beginning to end on one of my day's off. He'd told me that our blood circulating is what gives us color, keeps our nails and hair in place, and prevents our skin from ripping. "Death stops blood from pumping the pink to your cheeks. 'Orange' brings it back."

The mortuary hired a contract cosmetologist. Her name was Cindy, and she would paint the faces to look like a photo provided by the family and carefully brush their hair into styles that matched. But she was careful because if she wasn't, the hair would fall out into the brush, in clumps.

It was my job at night to turn off the lights and lock up the building. I was alone every night. I'd have to circle through the prep rooms with ten to a dozen bodies on tables in various states of undress, go through the viewing rooms and then lock up the chapel as well. Early on, I had decided that I would simply talk the whole time. To keep the creepiness out.

"Kingdom, Phylum, Class, Order, Family, Genus, Species."

"Just like a prayer, I'll take you there."

"If you drive a car eighty miles per hour, how long will it take you to get sixty miles?"

The only sound was my heels click-clacking on the tiled floors and my voice, loud, either singing or reciting words. Hoping to drown out the noise of the electronic air freshener you could find in every room that changed the chemical embalming smell to more of a chemical embalming lilac smell. The sound of the spray sometimes scared me when the buildings were empty of people who were alive.

The part I hated the most was walking through the long brick hallway between the office and viewing rooms to the chapel. It was dark, cold, and usually lined on either side with bodies in gurneys that had just arrived from the autopsy division. Often zipped in body bags or wrapped in stained sheets. These people would arrive at all times of day, usually when the coroners had some room in their schedule. They'd come through the back door, make a delivery, and then stop by upfront for a quick chat.

"Hey Diana, whatcha studying tonight?"

"Mostly my eyelids, but earlier it was about tectonic plates under the Middle East."

"Ugh, that sounds boring. Hey, I just made a delivery. Here's his paperwork. Stan Bradley, 24, strangulation."

"Are we doing the funeral or is it a cremation?"

"I don't know. The toxicology isn't back yet, so I doubt it's a cremation."

"Do they have suspects?"

"Not a murder."

"Suicide?"

"No."

"Wait, Darryl told me we had a guy last week from something called auto-erotica. Was that what he died of?"

"The report hasn't been made yet."

"I still think it's lame when you guys call that a suicide. It should be called an accident."

"I don't make the rules."

I had only been working a month when I walked a middle-aged woman to the largest of the cream-colored suites. Her daughter was lying inside a pewter casket. Bleach blond hair, teenage acne, and death by suicide. The funeral director was overbooked that Saturday and asked me to close the casket at the end of the viewing. I wasn't happy about it. I didn't feel qualified to be in charge of such a monumental moment for a family. They would never see her face again. Her mother stood staring down at her baby girl as I dropped the lid over her body and sealed it. She crumpled to the floor in her husband's arms and screamed, "Why didn't I listen?" over and over until he carried her out to their car in his arms. I watched through the window as he leaned over and put her seatbelt on.

In the year that I worked at the mortuary, there were maybe ten exclamation marks. A gang murder, a mother and daughter fighting over the cremation remains of a father and son, a Buddhist ceremony in our red-carpeted chapel, odd items found in bodies, and the day three pink dresses with matching rabbit jackets hung in the clothing booth.

I remembered hearing on the news about a local man who had stabbed his children to death the week prior. A man in the throes of a messy divorce. The dresses hung there next to the swinging door that led to the clinical white-walled room with four angled tables hooked up to tubes and drains. Those pink ribbons that hung around the hangers destined for the little girls' hair, was a clear and visual "Do not enter today" reminder to the staff. And I couldn't. I am and was a curious person, but I didn't need to be curious that day. I took a hard turn and headed back to my desk. There was an unspoken rule in the office. You never really spoke about the children. And when you cried silently, the other employees would touch your shoulder as they walked by to deliver flowers or organize the backhoe to dig the graves.

It wasn't always sadness. Most days and weeks were filled with elderly deaths. People who had families and had hopefully lived good lives—or so I hoped. The office and the break room and the prep rooms were like any job anywhere. There were pranksters, employee parties, inside jokes, and fun days. Every Saturday, six to ten bodies in a day might be buried or cremated, and all employees worked multiple funerals, multiple viewings. This was a job, not a lifestyle. Laughing was encouraged, but only in the break rooms. Learning the job was important. And I, an extraordinarily curious person who constantly hounded the funeral directors with biology questions, was the target of more jokes than others.

"Diana, oh my god, get back here, he's still alive!"

I only fell for that once.

"We need your help, his pants are too tight. When we slide him up, make sure his dick is straight or it might snap off."

"Shut up, you guys."

"No seriously, Darryl broke one off a few weeks ago."

"He did?"

And they howled in laughter.

Until that one night.

It was September. Still warm enough to not wear stockings with pumps. Still early enough in the evening for a bit of sunlight in that cool hallway that led to the chapel.

Click-clack click-clack. My shoes echoed off the brick walls.

"Goodnight, Mr. Wallace."

"Goodnight, Mrs., er, Hammond, Holland?" I attempted by reading the toe tag peeking out from under the sheets. "Someone has bad handwriting. Sorry. Goodnight, ma'am."

Click-clack click-clack.

Five more gurneys and I'm done saying goodnights.

Four...three...two...

IS THAT A HAND ON MY THIGH???

I froze. I couldn't scream. Or make a sound. In an emergency, apparently I will be the dumbass frozen in the middle of the fire. In that moment, in the silence of that hallway, the only sound was that of my pee filling up my right pump and dripping from my underwear onto the cement floor. Right before the coroner sat up from a gurney and pulled the sheet down from his face.

The next day when I arrived for work, the break room was decorated with roll upon roll of toilet paper.

{9}

Cheaper Heroin

The hostel in Sri Lanka was in the home of a woman of means. She'd been widowed during the civil war and gathered the wherewithal to turn her bedrooms into a backpacker hideaway in the Kandy Mountains. She was middle-aged with a gray braid, and she wore a white sari with gold trim that had flecked off from years of laundering against rocks in the local river. She made idlis and dhal for breakfast everyday for all the hostel guests.

There was a yoga couple from Holland who practiced complicated couple poses on the grass behind the house, and two young Japanese girls with their fresh Bangkok dreadlocks and Sanrio earphones. I had been on the road for nearly a year—hitching through Europe, playing cricket with glue boys in Nairobi, watching child weddings and camel trades in India—but I'd never hung out at a breakfast table with two English junkies who drooled globules of heroin-laced spittle onto their breakfast plates.

I'd seen this part of travel before. The drugs of the world. In Ecuador, I'd watched a young Norwegian man of maybe twenty buy heroin in a plaza overlooking the Pacific Ocean. All morning he'd been asking everyone in our hostel where he could score. We knew nothing of it, and with Columbia being only five miles away and this being 1996, we didn't want to know anything about it. That evening, he walked into an alley with three locals, I'm assuming purchased, and then disappeared. Never to be seen again.

In India, the heroin addiction seemed far more pronounced. The world's junkies, living on the dole from back home, bought black chunks of poppy paste for a fraction of the cost on their hometown streets. They could bunk in four dollar rooms together in Rajasthan, collect free needles from the hospitals, and shoot to their addiction's content. Sri Lanka was no different.

Only a month before, we'd met an elderly man with a yellow turban who asked if we wanted to eat with his family. We'd shared in their millet and goat, and then watched him drink his after-dinner poppy elixir and fade into an eye-rolled semi-consciousness while his wife, daughters, and granddaughters threshed more millet, milked the goats, and avoided my uncomfortable smile.

The drooling English couple at the table in Sri Lanka, in the home of Mrs. Ganoosh, shouldn't have surprised me. And yet I felt such disdain for their disrespect of our hostess's cooking, their disregard for the quietly known international language of smiling and hand gestures encouraged in *Lonely Planet* guidebooks. Instead, the bloated puffy Londoner and his emaciated track-riddled partner grabbed at their idlis with awkward hands and poked at their dhal, spilling it onto Mrs.

Ganoosh's plastic flowered tablecloth. They dropped the steamed rice discs to the floor, never making it close to their cracked and split lips and nourishing their young bodies with some much-needed toxic-cleansing lentils and spices. If only they could find their manners.

If only I could reach across the table and smack them upside their heads. Or if I could break into their rooms, find their passports, and call their families back home.

"Is your daughter Elizabeth Greenway?"

"She's here, in Sri Lanka by the way, and she looks like she's gonna live maybe another month."

I wondered what would happen to her body if this young English woman died at Mrs. Ganoosh's table in Sri Lanka. Who would dress her, and gather her wraparound skirts, worn Tevas, and rosewood bead necklaces, and package them up and send them all the way to Mr. and Mrs. Greenway back in Derbyshire? Would they cremate her, embalm her? Do they know how to embalm in Sri Lanka?

Maybe her family wouldn't care. Maybe I shouldn't.

Twenty years later in a hostel on the Pacific coast of Central America, I watched a German ex-pat drink himself to death. His name was Gerald, and the rumor around the hostel was that he was an Austrian college professor. He looked like an old weathered hippie who had lost so much weight his hip joints protruded. He'd sit on the couch at the hostel with his backpack and smile at the young travelers of the world while he poured endless swigs of rum into endless plastic cups of coke and ice. He never ate a thing. He never drank anything else. He was on his very own *Leaving Las Vegas*.

At a desolate gas station in the desert, somewhere in Baja Mexico, a young man with unplanned dreadlocks, filthy clothes, blue eyes, and no shoes asked me for a buck, in English, with no Spanish accent. He could have been my son. He could have been yours. Perhaps he didn't fit in from wherever he came from. Colorado or maybe New Hampshire. Perhaps he was mentally ill or got stranded as a drug mule. Perhaps he read *Into the Wild* and had chosen to drop out. What would happen to his body, his clothes, if he perished out there in the desert from dehydration or an overdose? Maybe that's what he wanted.

Perhaps not. But who am I to judge other people's journeys?

{10}

Well I Declare

I have a confession to make. I like my husband. A lot. And since I'm confessing, I'll also admit that I'm married to him, for realsies, and all my children carry his DNA. All of them. It's weird and old fashioned and something that in certain circles, I feel shy about. Shy, because I have nothing to offer in the way of partner bashing. Sometimes I even make shit up to be part of the clique. But even then, it's lame because it's usually about his socks stuck in our sheets or that he leaves water glasses all around the house.

"I mean seriously, he's such an ass. He leaves the drawers open in the kitchen...ALL THE WAY and then goes to work. Who does that? He's such a dick sometimes."

Twenty-one years is a long time to be with someone. But he's nice and kind, easy on the eyes, and can keep up with my constant banter about everything from twerking to tacos to *The Walking Dead*. He adds his own steampunk rants and fixie fixations while we eat eggs with hot sauce, listening to "A Prairie Home Companion," and discuss buying a VW in Germany for the ten-millionth time.

It started in college. Okay, high school, but really more like college. I got kicked out of San Juan High School for, uh, not going. Despite my endless efforts to rip off Macy's of their Ralph Lauren Polo shirts, I had managed not to fit in with anybody but the stoner crowd.

"Hey, where'd you get that shirt, maaaan?"

Somewhere during my sophomore year, I found out high school was slow and boring. I'm sure smoking a bowl in my VW in the school parking lot every morning before first period didn't help. By my junior year, the principal suggested I go to college instead and advocated an early start program for the gifted-but-can't-handle high school.

For a short time, I went through a snowboarder phase. I wore flannels over tank tops and baggy pants over my giant snowboard boots. I slept with guys who surfed in the summer and rode all winter. Their parties had as many bongs as beer, and we'd dance all night to Cypress Hill and toast our luck for figuring it all out so young.

The lights are blinkin' I'm thinkin'
It's all over when go out drinkin'

Until the snow melted and then everyone just looked kinda pale and weird in shorts and flip flops, and we moved onto other people and other parties.

My next party was a summer spent working on the beach and living in a VW van. My friend and I worked at a deli in a fancy town that had no summertime housing, so we'd park her bus on Highway 101 at a

Pacific overlook and steal showers at the local campground. Sometimes in the early mornings, I'd climb on the roof and watch the sunrise over the big blue ocean, writing endless journal entries about Mother Earth.

Usually a giant green station wagon parked near us with surfboards lashed to the roof. A guy I recognized from town by the name of Otter (or was it Turtle?) lived in it and worked as a bartender at the local pub. He'd wink at me every third beer, which he gave me for free. My radar told me it meant there would be certain expectations if I wasn't careful.

More often than not, there was another VW van pulled up alongside us. A two-tone, blue-and-white with a sunroof and 'Jake the Alligator Man' sticker on the back. I never saw the driver until the morning I smelled fried potatoes and saw smoke coming out of his sliding door.

Wondering what other homeless hippies had set up in their vans, I wandered over and came face-to-face with a blue-eyed long-hair cooking a tofu scramble with Jerry singing in the background. His name was Stevie, and his dog, Tahoma, sat behind him guarding her man with teeth bared. She acted every bit a jealous bitch.

"Hey, I'm Diana. I live in that green pickle van over there. How you doing this morning?"

"I'm good. I've seen you around town. I'd heard two girls were camping out for the summer in that thing."

"Yeah, we couldn't get a room anywhere, so this is home for now. You work in town?"

He said he flew kites for the local kite shop. For pay, he got a percentage of their day's profits and lived in his van at the University of Oregon during the school year. He studied geology and did contract work for an environmental consultant that required him to camp out in the woods sometimes for months at a time. It was just easier to stay in the van as a full-timer.

His van was clean. Lined with shelves of milk crates holding food and kitchen utensils. Breakfast was on a cast iron pan over a backpack stove that looked well-worn. I watched him pour on some Sriracha chili sauce when he was done and grab a fork from a tin cup bungeed to the back of his driver's seat.

It hadn't gone unnoticed that his Irish wool knit sweater hung on his huge shoulders just so. Or that his thigh muscles were as cut as an anatomy drawing. Or that his pearly white teeth kept popping out under a huge smiley face.

I didn't hear much of what he said that morning because it took every bit of energy for me not to overshare and pretend I liked the Dead. I concentrated on acting cool and aloof.

"Yeah, totally. I'm a bio major, third year. Just working the curve in case I wanna hit grad school, ya know?"

"Oh sweet, I just got a tat on my back, a little Mother Earth Gaia back there to remind me what's real, ya know?"

The whole summer we hung out, a big group of us from colleges all up and down the coast. We'd have drum circles on the beach, and I'd shake a dried bean pod trying not to stare at Stevie with his sun-bleached hair bouncing around his head as he grooved to the beats. We'd hike during the day and talk for hours about nudibranchs and magma-flow temperatures. Sometimes we'd argue, too, about Andy Warhol's tomato cans and how stupid they were, are, still.

Over time, I confessed I didn't like the Dead, or that I hated the Dead and their twenty-minute songs. I confessed I didn't understand *Watership Down* and had no desire to read *Siddhartha*. He smiled and told me he read sci-fi books and hated lentils. It was a moment. There were moments.

On Friday nights at the pub, there'd be live music, and I'd nurse beer after beer from a corner and watch him boogie down with the crowd until the floorboards screamed they were gonna burst. I'd watch the other broomstick skirt girls twirl around him with their belled bracelets and headwraps. Girls I'd curse under my breath, "Get the fuck away from him, Moondance, he's mine."

It wasn't until the last night of summer, when I was drunk off cheap beers, that Stevie finally squeezed my leg under the table. I saw the little sparkle in his eye and knew I was spending the rest of the night in his van.

Then he was gone. We all were. Back to school, back to late night papers, back to microbiology and Rachel Carson analysis. Something was different for me that year. I couldn't shake Stevie. I thought about him so much I stopped eating and ended up finding the campus therapist who spent four months talking through my feelings for that guy. It sucked so much that on a few Friday nights I'd sleep with a dumb-dumb just for the distraction. Guys named David and Scott who wanted to take me to breakfast the next day and tell me how "fuckin' wasted" they were in their market research classes.

One of them was kind of tolerable. He tried too hard but he would at least go backpacking with me, sometimes mountain biking. I would talk for hours about Edward Abbey's *Hayduke* and my obsession with Louise Erdrich. I'm not sure he ever understood what I was talking about, but he kept quiet and nodded at the appropriate times. He's what I needed to get over the boy in the van.

The sex sucked though. It was so bad because Sade was involved, and candles, too. To this day if I hear *The Sweetest Taboo* playing on an elevator, my vagina tries to grow another hymen to keep me from jumping in that bed again. Seriously, he bought "Rain" musk oil and would give me shitty backrubs in bubble baths with chilled champagne. I started to chew my arm off again until it was finally graduation.

I had had it by the end of school. What I wanted was freedom. Freedom to tramp around the country with a thumb and backpack. A month later, it got me to some Washington hot springs in a downpour that turned the roads to creeks, flooded my leather boots, and soaked my backpack to an amazing weight I couldn't carry anymore. Three hours in the rain, waiting for a ride. A ride that would get me out of the sea I was standing in.

I heard it before I saw it. Coming around the corner. There it was. A two-toned, blue-and-white VW van with a bitch of a dog in the front seat. When I opened the passenger door, he couldn't see that it was me with the hood of my coat over my head and a wool hat underneath.

But the second our eyes met while Jerry sang, "Goddamn, well I declare, have you seen the like," I knew my days pretending I was Sissy Hankshaw were over. I hopped in and threw my backpack next to the dog and then ejected the '74 show at Roosevelt Stadium out of the stereo while he smiled over at me.

"You got any real music in this VW?"

{11}

Bloody Camels

"**But I** didn't want to go to Morocco!"

"I know, baby."

"And I didn't want to go to the desert. Or ride a stupid camel or talk to that stupid French dude."

"I know. Here, you can use my handkerchief."

"It's too late, Steve. It's too late. I'm in a Muslim country covered in my own blood! I think there's stuff in the Koran about throwing rocks at me or something. It's everywhere!"

My husband had found me in a sand pit a hundred feet from a Bedouin tent in the middle of the Sahara desert. We had come to experience "The Nomadic Tribal Overnight Package." I'd woken up just that morning snuggled into my sleeping bag to the sound of nearby camels bickering and felt the early twinges of my monthly cramps.

Before anyone was awake in our fanciful tent, a large structure made of tree branches and blue fabric with a floor covered in Asian rugs, I'd rustled around in my day bag for a shred of pink toilet paper. We hadn't paid for the deluxe experience. You had to bring your own water, toilet paper, snacks, clothes, and all of it had to fit into one very small bag. Therefore, my ziplock with a year's worth of OB tampons was locked up safe and secure back at the hostel. But the mighty dam had broken early, thanks probably to a five-hour journey on a camel the day before.

If you haven't ridden on the back of a camel, let me tell you, it's not like a horse. You don't straddle it and hang on with your thigh muscles. Instead you sit any possible way you can without falling off. Cross-legged, on your stomach, on your back. The saddle is merely a platform with blankets, and it rocks you back and forth through the soft sand. I had spent most of the day trying to keep my lips from cracking and my body from falling off six feet in the air. My stomach muscles had worked a thousand crunches just trying to keep me upright on that topsy-turvy saddle. Somewhere in the process, I had massaged my uterus walls and convinced it to shed early and bountifully.

When I walked out of our tent in the early morning, I already knew there was no bathroom. Only miles of sand bumps and dips. If I was going to drop my drawers within eyeshot of the camel herders, our guide, and the cook, I'd need to find a big dip in the sand. To hide my ass in. It took fifty steps. By the time I found a place, there was blood to my knees. I'm sure most people would have assumed I'd miscarried. It looked like a scene from a horror movie.

By the time I got to a dip big enough and squatted down, it was now just for the pure enjoyment of watching beetles crawl out of the sand and attack the already drying puddle of urine I'd left behind. I had no need for toilet paper. It was that arid. In seconds, it drip-dried all of my clothes, underwear, and body.

"What am I going to do?"

"There's nothing you can do. Tie your shirt around your waist."

Steve had woken up and come to look for me. He found me crying over the sand with my pants and underwear around my ankles. The blood was now dry and crisp on my legs and twat. It was hardened to my khakis. Hard-ened. Like they were stiff.

I read once that a woman's period is six teaspoons of blood. Mine was a cup. I probably needed a transfusion.

The tears dried on my cheeks before they reached my lips. The snot in my nose cracked and mixed with more of my blood. I had no idea what to do. I had nothing to change into. I would have to wear my stiff clothing for the rest of the day riding on that camel back to Zahara. I made a pad out of my husband's handkerchief, tied my only long-sleeve shirt around my waist, and headed back for leftover tajine with our guide—an arrogant twenty-something from Marrakesh who did nothing but flirt with the other two female guests.

The previous evening, when I'd been blood-free, I'd conversed using hand signals and loud English to find out the recipe for the chicken stew we ate for dinner. It had green olives, carrots, cardamom. The cook was kind and played along. "Is that coriander seed?" I asked. He set aside samplings of each spice for me to taste and write down in my journal. He was a Bedouin, had grown up nomadic, and had only recently given up that lifestyle to work with tourists. He came to the company with his own camel, the one I'd ridden on to get to our tent in the desert. He was caring, unlike our guide who left in a Mercedes claiming to be much too busy for the return camel journey.

With lots of Steve's encouragement, I eventually joined our group now stretching and drinking tea inside our blue tent. I walked awkwardly with my hands in front of me, legs crossed, and managed to settle on the carpets with a pillow on my lap. The cook handed me sweet mint tea with some bread. He looked me right in the eyes and gave me a sympathetic smile. I'm sure dried tears on top of my facial road dust left a perfect map of my morning out in the Sahara Desert.

When it was time to return to our camels, the cook helped me back onto his own personal camel. He offered me a knee to climb up and then his shoulder, so I could hoist a leg over the stacked blankets. There I sat for five more hours rocking back and forth on the blanket, feeling each drip drop of my uterus lining staining the cook's Bedouin blankets.

{12}

Tweaking

Ryder had been born for a whole ten minutes before my parents walked in the front door with a video camera turned on. I was in the back bedroom holding my nine-pound bundle of joy, while my legs hung over the side of the bed and my twat hovered over a large bowl on the floor. The video shows two midwives down on their knees staring at my canal and gently tugging on an umbilical cord still inside my body.

I see my parents enter the room, and I smile a brilliant smile at them and the camera. "Look at the baby!" I yell, pointing at this thing while so high on endorphins I don't even know what's happening around me. You don't notice the baby in my arms because the room is filled with equipment and towels, and there's a streak of blood on the wall, and the mattress is soaked red, and it's all you notice in the video.

The camera just keeps rolling. My parents say nothing. *At all.* My mother-in-law had been at the birth, and for some reason had called my parents within one minute and told them to come fast from the hotel.

If I'd been on my game, I'd have insisted on being cleaned up first. It just happened. So I'm sitting there on the side of the bed, naked with my baby, the midwives tugging on the umbilical cord, and then they reach up and start tweaking my nipples like a dial from an old radio. In front of my Dad. Tweak tweak. Tweak.

The camera never pauses.

The goal was to get the placenta out because I'm a bleeder. They were trying to stimulate it out. I smiled at my baby in bliss, holding him close to my enormous boobs while people worked on my nether-regions.

The camera finally turns out of the room in silence and heads down the hallway. My step-father's footsteps are heard in the background. He stops in the kitchen, puts the camera down on the counter, and it focuses on my dining room wall. The only sound is his intensely heavy breathing. Then a giant sigh. Then he turns the camera off.

{13}

Sandwich Wrappers

Laurie's mouth formed words, something to do with an auction, and another Mama named Jenny nodded her approval. Our children ran around nearby, back and forth from the playground to the healthy picnic of hummus and carrots, and grapes and almonds that was spread out over an unstained red-and-white checkered cloth. I heard the Mamas' voices and paid attention as best I could. It had become more difficult as of late to follow all the rules. I kept telling myself I just needed to try harder but instead found myself more interested in the small barren oak tree, the only one in our manicured park. The only oak in a park surrounded by maples.

"So they auctioned off five reuseable sandwich wraps, and Jenny and I couldn't stop our bidding war." Laurie is dark, tan before summer, with shiny healthy glowing black hair I assume comes from drinking water, lots of it over a lifetime.

Laurie's BFF Jenny, sat with perfect posture from yoga on Saturday mornings, hair pulled in a tight bun.

"I totally wanted those things! I hate washing out Aidan's Tupperware everyday."

Aiden's Tupperware. Again. I'm sure the miniature plastic tubs are filled with homemade whole grain mini-muffins and figs she probably dried herself last summer, from her own tree. I pictured him at school, with seven Tupperwares on the cafeteria table, lids placed carefully underneath each piece with a napkin laid out in front to catch the crumbs. I'm sure Aiden would hate to leave a mess for the custodian at school.

"So the woman who runs the auction just kept going back and forth and back and forth while Jenny and I kept upping our bids by a quarter." Laurie moved her fingers through her dazzling hair, her thin bony hands with clear fingernails, probably from the water, too.

Breathe, I told myself. Breathe.

I lay back on my park sheet I always keep in the trunk, stained with cherry juice and oil from something, somewhere. I should have washed it over the winter, but I never seem to remember that kind of stuff. The Mamas would have remembered.

I look at the lonely oak. I've noticed that it never drops its brittle dry leaves until the new ones bud out in springtime. All winter it hangs on tightly to those leaves, maroon mottled brown, twirling in the wind, hanging on and waiting for new life.

"So I offered five dollars and ten cents and then Jenny started wavering." Laurie throws a wink over towards her bestie Mama friend. They've begun to dress alike with their rolled up jeans and gray cardigans, sporty sandals for hiking with off-road strollers.

"I saw them for sale at Village Merchant on Division, and I thought, 'I don't know, they're getting kind of expensive.'"

How many Wednesdays had we talked about the auction, before the auction? Now we're talking about it, after the auction. I didn't go to the auction. I didn't go to the stupid auction raising money for goats or bark chips or some paint for an outbuilding for hula hoops or balls. Nope, I read a trashy Kindle book I bought for ninety-nine cents on Amazon. Took me six hours to read it. Seventeen cents an hour.

"Well, finally, Lisa pounded the gavel, and I had won the lot for five dollars and twenty-five cents," Jenny declared.

"I'm so jealous now. They were soooo cute, red flannel with cars and tractors. I think she makes them for her Etsy shop."

Do people really make money from their Etsy shops? Or is it a hobby like knitting that they've turned into a job description? "Oh, I can't work at the auction, I've got my Etsy shop to take care of." Like, do Etsy shops make go-to-Europe money? I'd like to go to Paris this summer with my husband. I want to walk at midnight, make out near a fountain, and have sex in an alley somewhere, dark from foggy streetlights.

"Ryder, remember, we only go up the stairs and down the slide," says Laurie, using her rules on MY son.

I stop daydreaming of raunchy sex in Paris and sit up, take notice. Do my bit to show I'm paying attention. I care. Up the ladder, now down the slide. Right, this is what the good Mamas do. I watch my son as he looks over at our clutch, not really hearing all of Laurie's words. I shake my head, subtly, but enough for him. He knows now, today, this moment, there are rules. He's learning socialization. I'm learning socialization. We're learning to conform.

Laurie turns back her lustrous head of hair with her best "sweet boy" look on her face, proud she taught my son how to play the right way. "So Jen, I tried that recipe you gave me for the homemade tofu pâté. It's so delicious. Mark just loves it. It's so easy." BFFs exchange recipes after teaching children how to play. Note taken.

I close my eyes and remember the feta salads in Spain with eggs and green wine that we ate after hard days of work on the olive farm. Was there a recipe somewhere out there for those salads? Did it include the smoke from the bread oven nearby, or the sound of German and English chatter about the best way to infuse lavender? Would they still be so good in this park right now, with these Mamas I've tried so hard to be like?

"I know, right?" Jen pops a perfect green grape in her mouth, taken from more Tupperware with lids that match and fit and stack and have no spaghetti stains in them. "I had to make about ten different recipes until I felt like it was a pretty good pâté. Now I put it in Aiden's lunches with rice crackers, and we have it for snacks after school with homemade pita bread."

Celery salt, I heard that detail last week. The pâté. It needs celery salt. That's the secret the Mamas had said. But then I asked, "How do you make celery salt? Why do you make celery salt? Who made the first celery salt?" The Mamas had giggled at my outburst. I wonder if the first celery salt maker knew that one day they'd rule the Moms at the park with newfangled salt. I couldn't stop thinking, is celery salt supposed to be ironic?

They're quiet now, the Mamas, in their sun hats they bought at REI for fifty bucks. Worried about skin cancer, they threw it in their baskets on a whim, after trying on a new pair of KEENs for a hundred. Do they know they are celery salt? Watery celery mixed with dehydrating salt? Bidding at auction for sandwich wrappers while wearing KEENs? Do they even know what I would mean if I said that? Or would it just be me again, bringing up more fodder for their Friday night double dates? When Laurie and Jenny explain to their husbands how awkward I am at the park when I randomly recite a passage from Sandra Cisneros' *The Mango Tree.* Do they know, that I know that their husbands will only half-listen to their conversation because they're distracted by the waitress with giant tits. Because why not? Giant tits and a beer has got to be more interesting than celery salt and what I did at the park on Wednesday.

I kinda wanna yell that I don't want to make sandwiches that need wrappers. I don't like sandwiches. I like Indian food with a cold Pepsi. Chicken tikka with a side of pakoras. Like I used to eat on the sides of the dirt roads in Bengal and Rajasthan, on a motorcycle, before the mindless days in this park with tofu pâté and homemade sandwich wrappers.

Is there a Mama in India right now, sitting in a park with chapatis and dhal listening to chatter about homemade pesto? Is she staring up at a jacaranda tree now, wondering if it's native to the Himalayan Basin region?

Does she wonder if this is it? If she's made the wrong choice, signed up for the wrong club? Is she looking for me in amongst all those yellow saris? Because I'd like to find her one day. Maybe we'll laugh together when we feed our kids idlis with peanut butter and jelly while they run up the slides and down the ladder.

{14}

Dear Diana

I figured it out at Ronald's funeral. About Mom, that is. After forty-five years, it took someone else's funeral to open my eyes. I sat in the front pew holding her hand, trying to protect her from her ex who might show up that afternoon to say goodbye to his best friend, horizontal in the casket. The two men had been friends for seventy years, and my father had been told to stay away from the funeral, because Mom would be there to support the newly widowed. Her best friend of seventy years.

> *Dear Diana,*
> *I want to start by apologizing for not being in your life.*
> *Your Mother kept me away. She's not the angel you think she is.*

Mother is petite, thin, and almost frail-looking sometimes. She plays dumb in front of men with her big blue eyes surrounded by soft peach skin. She plays dumb despite her multiple degrees and successful careers. I see it. I'm aware. It's her suit of armor. It's her protection against wrath.

The funeral was expected. My godfather had been dying for three long years from lung cancer after a well-lived life full of parties and friends and children and marriage. My mom thought Marlene should have left Ronald years ago when he was drinking. And then drinking. Then drinking again. She should have left him like Mother left Father. Then another father after that.

"She shouldn't have had to put up with that," Mom would say.

Marlene is my Godmother, my mother's BFSTTG—Best Friend Since The Third Grade. Two best friends who married two best friends.

Marlene doesn't wear a suit of armor. She asks pointed questions. She talks about her son's drug problems openly; she talks about Weight Watchers, about puppies and babies and marriage. She loves my mother. She's her best friend. They are best friends. They're very different.

Dear Diana,
I believe in my sobriety, and I believe in myself. I want to repair the damages my drinking has caused. You have no idea how much I wanted to meet you when you were younger, but your Mother wouldn't allow it.

We sat in an Arby's when I was thirteen, sharing fries, when she told me I had another father. That the life I knew up to that point wasn't really the whole story.

"I married a man named Alan when I was twenty-five. He's your father. Not Bill. Bill adopted you when you were five years old, and we told you he was your father. Now he's gone so you should know the truth."

We always went to Arby's after my weekly counseling sessions. Her violent divorce from Bill, apparently husband number two, had taken a toll on me, and the silent tears I shed had worn me down, exhausted me. Mother was already with future husband number three and hadn't noticed my exhaustion or sadness until I took a bottle of aspirin and sleeping pills and woke up in the intensive care unit at Kaiser. I didn't see her for days after that until my required counseling sessions began. She had been too broken up to be near me. Her new boyfriend drove me from the hospital to my aunt's house to finish "recovering" from my overdose. He had shielded her from the pain that was me.

"Did you hear me, Diana? Bill is not your father."

"I heard you."

I felt embarrassed. I thought about all the times I told people I'd gotten my allergies from Dad and that I wanted to grow up and be a scientist, like Dad. Now it turned out, everybody around me, even my perfect cousins with perfect hair and perfect swim trophies, knew that Bill wasn't my real dad. Everybody knew, but me, until this day at Arby's.

"If you ever want to know anything about your real father, ask your godmother. She knows him. She's still friends with him. She'll tell you whatever you want to know. Including where he is. But I won't talk about him. Ever again."

And that was that. Never another word about Alan. Or Bill. They were both gone from our lives and never to be mentioned again. Except in my counseling appointments. With strangers.

> *Dear Diana,*
> *I want you to know I am considered very smart amongst*
> *my friends. I golf every day and have been clean and sober*
> *for six months now.*

During the funeral, three men I'd never met stood up and introduced themselves as my godfather's best friends since childhood. My real father had been part of their band of five, wreaking havoc on their Oakland neighborhood in the 1940s and '50s. They told their stories in front of a packed funeral house. These old men in sports jackets with ties. Wiping tears from their eyes between chuckles. How they had played baseball in the streets together, rode bikes to the pier, stole candy from the corner market. They still, to this day, get together. Two hundred people watched these three men laugh and cry and celebrate Ronald's life. The fourth member, not there.

I held Mom's hand while these guys told their stories. They mentioned Dad by name. Probably the first time in my life I'd ever heard him mentioned in a group or whispered under breaths. Everyone around me knew she'd shut Alan out. He had given up his parental rights. They knew more about all of it than I did, sitting in the front row holding hands with half the story.

"He's a con man," my godmother had told me when I was about twenty-two, years after I'd learned he even existed. College roommates wondered if he had more children, and I realized I didn't even know. Maybe I wasn't an only child. "He's smart as hell, good looking, and smooth, but that's it. It's all he's got."

My godmother gave me his phone number in case I wanted to talk to him. "Be careful." Which I was. And it was awkward.

"Do you have really long toes?" he asked.

"Yeah, I do. Sometimes people comment on them."

"Good, I just wanted to make sure you were mine."

Son of a bitch. That son of a bitch didn't just add that to the story, did he? Make it all more complicated by suggesting he might not be my father? That son of a bitch wasn't going to talk that way about Mother. I didn't speak to him again.

The gathering after the funeral took place at my godmother's house. I took it upon myself to serve wine and clean up the kitchen while my godmother sat with her friends and family and laughed at funny stories about her husband. Ronald had always been such a nice guy. Drunk or not, he was a nice guy. But I didn't know what to do there at the house. The room was filled with people I never knew. They all shared history, so I filled up wine glasses for men who stared at me. Maybe they would be reporting on me at the monthly golf game to my father. I've seen his photo. I'm clearly his daughter.

My mother was already at home in her pajamas. She had looked like a lamb at slaughter after the funeral, surrounded by a past that she'd forgotten or pushed away or tidied into a neat package called "before." A past she was done with the moment it passed.

Dear Diana,
I have a wife and step-daughter who love me. They give me cards on Father's Day.

While I wiped the counters in the kitchen after the funeral, a woman approached me with tears in her eyes and a tissue in her hand. "Thank you," she said.

"Oh, it's no problem. I don't mind." I rinsed off a serving dish.

"No, thank you for coming today. It meant a lot to his friends. The ones who spoke? They were upset that Alan couldn't, well, he couldn't come say goodbye to his friend."

I knew who she was. I had spent enough time over the years sitting in clutches of white wine women to know the black sheep when I saw her. Long hair without a style, almost to her butt, bright colors at a funeral, big hoop earrings. She was the one who had known the boys since the old days in Oakland. The younger sister who knew all the secrets. Had tagged along and followed the gossip throughout all of their lives. They had mentioned her in their funeral side stories. Gloria was her name. Without much thought, I was certain my mother felt uncomfortable near her. This woman was real, and she was going to get real.

"He wanted to be here, you know."

"I'm assuming you're talking about Alan."

"I am. Your dad loved these guys his whole life. I talked to him this morning. He wanted you to know that if he could have come, he would have."

"Well, I'm sorry. I don't understand the history of all this. I don't know the stories. I only know my mother, and she was scared he would come today."

"Your mother loves you. She just wants to protect you."

"Maybe. I'm a grown woman though with three kids of my own. I don't feel like I need protecting."

"Sure you do. We all do."

She reached over and touched my hand, and I looked at her glossy brown eyes. They were kind and sympathetic. I didn't look away. I forced myself to keep my eyes on her for longer than I felt comfortable. I wanted her to know *me*. That I wasn't *my mother*.

"No. I could have handled it, if he was here today. I think he should have been. I think maybe Mom shouldn't have come instead. I get that.

Alan deserved to be here. Today was about Ronald. Not my mother."

"That's kind of you to say, Diana. He loves you no matter what."

"That's nice. I guess."

Dear Alan,
I received your letters. I see you are in a twelve-step program.
I hope it helps you find peace in your life. You don't owe me
an apology though because I don't know you. You didn't hurt
me. I've had a good life.

You hurt Mother. I believe you owe her an apology for whatever
you did and then you need to forgive her for whatever she did
to you. People shield her from that which is painful, so you will
never get closure. You will never make peace with her, but you
have no need to make peace with me. Rest assured, Alan, I live
my life with open eyes.

{15}

Blowjob Club

If there's only one piece of advice I'd give any young woman in a hetero relationship, especially if she's had a child, it's this: Give more blowjobs. I'm serious. I started the Blowjob Club a few years ago when I noticed my Mama friends were "holding out" because of an under-the-skin resentment toward their partners that happens when you have kids. You're tired, you haven't showered, the kids have been all over your body all day long. The idea of getting durdy with your partner sounds exhausting. So I started the BJ club. Here's why.

When you're living the Groundhog Day of family life, sitting on the couch watching TV night after night after the kids have been put to bed, a couch BJ takes one commercial break. This is a Wednesday night, folks, and the most exciting thing that's happened to him all week is when someone brought in bagels to the office as a thank you for a quick turnaround on that quarterly report. The shock and awe of his partner unzipping his comfy jeans while he listens to the side effects of an allergy medicine during a commercial break, means three minutes is all it's gonna take.

By the way, it's Garbage Day. Did you know that? There's milk in the fridge, too, that he picked up on the way home after nine hours on the job. He also has really crappy shoes because he never takes the time to shop for himself. He spends most of his time working or with you. Three minutes, friends.

Plus you haven't showered all day. You're in your sweats. You can do this one thing for him with a fucking ponytail! It's like it was made for tired, stressed-out moms. I mean, how hard is it to say some dirty words, too? Spice it up in the shock-and-awe department. It's a BJ, nature's mysterious evolutionary sex cousin. Do it.

Maybe you're thinking, "But what about me?" Did you want to be part of the sex club? If you won't give a couch BJ because it sounds like a gift to your man laid out on a fluffy pink pillow, then you might wanna understand what gift giving is all about. Yes, this is all about him. Kinda.

Men must ejaculate or their balls turn blue and fall off. Which means, if you don't couch-BJ it, he's jacking off somewhere in your house and dirtying up a sock. What do you think he's jacking off to? I'll take a guess it's Ashley Madison. Or Pornhub. Or some other site turning his phone into a virus magnet.

Guess what they do on those sites? Um, blowjobs. Dirty durdy blowjobs. Which is what he's thinking about when you shrug him off again, because you're tired. He wants you, always has. Shrug. He loves you, so he's kind and waits. Shrug. He does everything in his power to be a good husband, father, son, and man. Shrug.

I mean, he might not be really into it. You're right. I mean he probably totally understands your consistent shrugs. I don't know. I've only been with my husband for twenty-three years. I do know though that you love him. Or did. And maybe you forgot how to show it. Not sure.

But is it gonna hurt? Is it gonna ruin your relationship or mess with your *Bachelorette* recap coming right up? It could. But probably not. It only takes a few minutes to find out.

{16}

Fridays

I sit in my twenty-year-old VW parked in front of my job site, defeated and sobbing. The car is making a new cling-clang noise on the way over, and I'm not sure I can take anymore this week. How much will it cost to make the cling-clang go away? Deep down, I know I'm crying because I'm hungry and exhausted and more scared than I've ever been in my life, so I allow just a few minutes of uncontrolled fear to come out through my tears before I have to be the confident boss lady handing out Friday paychecks.

You see, I've gambled my family's entire future on this year's plan, and I'm currently in deep, really deep, $750,000 deep. I haven't eaten much in two days because food tastes like metal and because my children need to eat first. My stomach is in knots most days anyway while I run from job site to job site, calculating losses, ordering materials, fighting down bids, hurrying crews, making offers, and checking on my kids via texts.

Sometimes, I puke by the side of the road, and it feels fantastic afterward. All the worry and fear and anger spews out in my bile, and I feel refreshed for a few hours. They don't need to know that part. The guys on my job site. They can't know how badly I'm stretched to the limit, or their trust in me will be lost, and they won't show up for work Monday morning.

So I clamp it down. I dry my eyes and take some deep breaths while staring at myself in the rearview mirror.

"It's just business, this is just business," I say out loud, reminding myself half-heartedly that nobody in my family is dying. It's been three years since we've had a job. Since everyone lost their jobs. We're still here, together. Just homeless and hungry. It could be worse.

I finger-pick my hair and check my teeth for black beans before I try on a smile. It looks fake, but it's good enough.

"You can do this," I say out loud. Confidence is the language these men speak. I must exude it, or they'll sniff me out, and I don't have time for nervous breakdowns right now.

I open the door into the cold winter sunlight and change my shoes into rubber work boots for the muddy pathways around my construction project. This house had been abandoned for two years before I bought it with borrowed cash from a private lender and gutted down to the studs. The neighbors came out and thanked us when we put in new doors and windows. Their own yards had been littered with garbage over the years from homeless encampments in the backyard and the living room. The constant parade of people coming and going, drug deals, drunken late night fights, had worn this neighborhood down. They kept closer eyes on their children, checked their bushes for needles. I wonder what they would think of my homeless kids riding scooters up and down the street in front of our RV. Are we of a higher caste homeless?

"Hey Ramone. ¿Cómo estás?" I say walking up toward the front door.

"Deannnna, Deannnnna, Deannnnna, mi amor," he says carrying a four-by-four of HardieBacker in his arms, a black tool belt around his waist, set off by his favorite University of Oregon gray hoodie.

Ramone is my favorite, with his green eyes and gold-toothed smile. He walked to Portland from Chiapas in 1995 to pick blueberries and send money home to his pregnant wife. He survived in rest areas, sleeping under bushes, and begging food off of travelers along I-5 on the way. He eventually taught himself framing, decking, trim, and fences over the years by watching *This Old House* with Bob Villa. Now he's my most reliable asset.

"Ramone, did you move that beam over a quarter inch?"

"Yes, maaaaa'aaaam, we did."

"All right, just checking before the rockers come on Monday."

Ramone's wife and two boys still live in Mexico. They live on a goat ranch he bought for them ten years ago in Oaxaca. He spends a month a year down there, building a hacienda big enough for his parents and cousins. He loves his family and goats and his boys who are studying to be police officers.

"I told you, Deanna, we'd finish by noon today. It'll be done. Don't you worry."

"Then when it's ready for Miguel, take off early if you want."

Because they're paid hourly. I need them to take off. I need to save money wherever I can to keep them afloat in the long run, to keep us all afloat. This endeavor I started a year ago, when our unemployment was drying up, when we were forced to move into an RV. Ever an opportunist, I had asked my husband over breakfast one day if he would be willing to put our house up as collateral against an idea I had spinning in my head. I was gonna flip houses, lots of them, as many as I could until we could breathe, eat, and sleep soundly.

"Ramone, here's your check. Make sure you buy Lupita that Boer buck she wanted and have her send photos. I wanna see this famous Chiapas prize-winner."

"I worry, Deanna, what if she falls in love with him more than me?" He giggles at his own joke before he passes out paychecks to his guys, Nato and Leo.

Fridays are always a good time in construction. Cashed checks pad their wallets with dollars for nightclubs, for rent, for groceries, beer. Another week they have proof they are done hauling out moldy sheetrock, piss-laden carpets, and crack pipes that fill our dumpsters to the overflowing. The cold and the rain and the mud, they never complain about. They are sons of construction, grandsons. They know little else for employment, and the weather is simply their office. So Fridays are a good day for everybody but the boss lady who's running out of cash if something doesn't change soon.

"Hey, Aaron," I nod toward my tiler. He's busy on his hands and knees with earplugs in to keep his cutting numbers straight in his head. Two-and-five-eighth by an eleven-and-a-quarter with a two-and-a-quarter by a three-and-a-quarter cut on southwest corner. One tile at a time, every piece different numbers.

I met Aaron a few days after his wife left him. He's the tallest of the crew with curly brown hair and a three-day beard that he scratches at when he's nervous. Which is always. His wife worked at the hospital when I was treated for a gallbladder attack after two of my deals went sour in one afternoon, and I thought I was having a heart attack. She had seen my job title on my paperwork and told me he'd been unemployed for nearly a year. Like most people in this business, the economic crash left many relationships broken and defeated, even bankrupt. As soon as I hired Aaron over the phone, she left him.

"I need more grout by Monday," he says when he looks up from the floor with clear eye goggles over his dark gray eyes. He should have had enough for the job. I'd calculated it out myself.

"Okay, but I'm only getting one more bag. You're dumping a lot in the garbage pile; mix less or buy your own bags. You got it?"

Aaron nods and turns back to the 185 tiles he has to install by five. I leave his paycheck on the tile pile, a hundred dollar bonus toward his plane ticket home to Minnesota for his nephew's wedding next month. A hundred dollars I don't really have, but I worry he won't come back. His wife will be at the wedding. I don't want his heart to break in half. I need him to think about Portland, about coming back home after that wedding. I have more tile I need set for the next house.

His dog, Atticus, comes running over to me, nuzzles my hand for a treat. I always keep them in my pocket for the crew dogs or for my kids to give the crew dogs, and Atticus knows it. I think his big blue eyes and chocolate fur are the only thing getting Aaron through this cold winter.

"Oh, big boy, whatcha doing, big boy?" I bend down to hug the pit bull, his tail pounding on my arm while he licks my face. Aaron smiles over at us, always watchful on his big boy.

"Hey Princess!" comes a yell from outside. My sider Alex from the Ukraine is still on the site after too many weeks.

"Whadaya want, Alex?" I yell from hugging Atticus, stealing his warmth through my hoodie.

"When you can spare me a minute, almighty one, get out here and let me know how-how-how you want this facia."

His stutter is intense. Sometimes he can't even speak. Phone conversations are impossible, and I have to meet him in person on site for discussions, and even then, we use paper and pen. He used to be worse, but he's gotten used to me and doesn't get so nervous now.

His long red beard sits under his swollen nose and glassy yellowing eyes. I hand him his paycheck, which will surely disappoint. His son's college tuition is due this month, and he's been hinting all week for a bigger draw from his $12,000 bid.

"Why so little, Princess?"

"Because you're still not fuckin' done, Alex."

I can smell the drink on him this morning. BENGAY is what they all blame it on, the ones that day drink. That's why he gets here at nine thirty every morning instead of seven. If I pay him too much during the project, he won't show up for a week. He'll binge.

"Oooh, I love it when you talk to me like that, Princess." He smiles hard toward me with those cirrhosis eyes and then turns away when I match his stare.

"Before I forget, Alex, stop calling my husband to place orders. You know I place the orders. I sign the checks, yeah?"

"Well, I'm not making orders with women, only men." He's referring to my geometric challenge; I can't see things 3D. I simply don't use that part of my brain, and Alex knows it from all the times he's tried to explain why my idea won't work, why I can't have a belly band at the front porch line, or why the cement pad and stairs are a quarter inch off.

"I get your point, I do. But hear me, Steve's overworked with rentals right now, don't be bugging him on flips. You go through me only, you got it? If I need interpretation, I'll ask Steve."

"Ya know, Princess, Steve wouldn't be so stressed if you'd let him go to the titty bars." His buddy, Paul, laughs behind me, always with a cigarette dangling from his lips.

"I'd be at the titty bar way before Steve and you know it, cocksucker. Now shut the fuck up and shoot that facia from the underside so I can't see the nails, you hear me asshole?"

"You got it, Prin-Prin-Princess," he says, always *always* with a smile as I sweep past him, Paul throwing me a high-five.

"You're a dick," Paul mumbles toward Alex while I head back inside to check my phone.

Three texts. One from my son asking if they can walk to the store and buy milk.

Of course, honey. Take the laundry money in the jar above the sink.

The second text is from my realtor. An offer coming in on a house that's been sitting on the market for three months. If all goes well in inspection, we could close in five weeks and give me some much needed cash to keep paying these guys. Maybe my seven credit cards can hold us until then.

I measure out for cabinets in the kitchen. I'm going with Quaker maple with a granite countertop from Margaret. My kids call her dragon lady because she draws Chinese dragons on their hands with a Sharpie pen and gives them fortune cookies from under her countertops. Her family cuts granite in Shanghai, and they ship it to San Francisco, Seattle, and Portland. She has a sibling in each city drawing dragons on little boys' hands. I'll call her later when I check the balances on my cards, find some credit in there to buy a kitchen and a bathroom.

Call me when you can.

It's from my husband, currently overhauling a rental we bought with our flip profits, all cash. Before I call him, I walk away from the saws and the wood piles and tile to the master bathroom with its new Jacuzzi tub that cost me $1,200. I sit inside the empty tub and dial my husband's number.

"Hey, how are you, you okay?"

"Yep, I'm fine," I say. "I'm at 65th paying the boys. Got a text from Kyle that 92nd has an offer coming in."

"Whew, couldn't be more timely, am I right?"

"Yeah, I think we've got about $5,000 to our names after the boys cash their checks this week. Not sure how I'm going to pay them next week."

I can hear Steve thinking. He never really knows our finances but just assumes we're always broke, which is a safe bet because I won't let us touch any flip money for a few years. The plan is to keep buying keepers or rentals until we have enough income to live off of. "You'll figure it out, you always do."

"I will," I say.

"Hey, you okay?" Just that morning we'd shared a can of black beans with some leftover rice, salt being our only condiment. I knew why he was worried. I didn't talk the entire time I ate, which is usually impossible.

"Yep, something will give. We haven't worked this hard for nothing. One day, it'll all make sense." I rub my forehead and block my eyes from the skylight above the tub. I want to hide in this tub forever, curl up, and just sleep. Pretend like I don't have kids and employees and debt and responsibilities bigger than I can handle. I've got seven houses right now, one forty-foot RV, three growing boys, a husband, and eight employees. I also realize I need a tampon and a toilet in a room with an actual door.

"It will. We're gonna be fine Diana, you know that, right? You're doing it, it's working, it's all working."

"I guess I do. It's just..."

"I know. But tomorrow is a new day, and it'll feel new. For now, buy an Almond Joy, splurge. It's Friday for you, too."

"Thanks, babe, but only if you buy a Reese's though. Deal?"

"Deal."

{17}

Barrio

My family built a house for a woman in Central America who was raising six kids on four dollars a day by selling handmade tortillas cooked over an open fire in her backyard. I was embarrassed to share this with my friends in the States, even though my kids raised the money for materials. I didn't want to tell anyone I knew that we would be building this house for a family in another country. It felt very White Girl Saving The World. As if I knew better. As if I was the Duchess helping out the tenants. As if I knew how others should live.

During the days on the jobsite, we worked and sweated in the barrio. My husband and my three sons. The barrios had no running water. Every block or so there was a spigot like you might have in your backyard for watering your garden. People would spend all day filling up water jugs and laundry buckets, walking back and forth to their ramshackle huts they built from whatever they could find in the streets. After a few weeks of mixing cement, carrying brick, sifting sand, losing gallons of sweat, we left this woman with so few possessions and so many mouths to feed with a metal roof, four brick walls, two doors, one window, and a dirt floor. But it didn't feel good. It gave me a bitter taste in my mouth because I couldn't do more for her and her family. I couldn't really change anything except maybe her safety. And then only mildly.

Before we'd gone to Central America for this adventure, I'd been in contact with the organization that matched us with a woman in need. The staff person running the program told me over and over again we wouldn't survive staying in the barrio. I'd asked her if we could rent a room from someone there. "You'd be more comfortable staying in Granada. Rent a house. There are plenty on Airbnb."

We already had a lot of experience volunteering internationally. We'd always made it a point to stay where we volunteered or at least rent rooms nearby from a local family. We had experience with rats and mice and cockroaches in our rooms. In Thailand and Malaysia, Guatemala, and Mexico. I wanted my kids to spend time living like others in the barrio, surrounded by kids their ages who played games with wooden tops and killed lizards for entertainment. Okay, maybe I didn't want that part but...I wanted them to live just like the kids in the barrio for a month. To remember that feeling when we came back home to the States and our three bedroom home in Portland, and they told me they were bored surrounded by excess.

Instead, I followed the directions from the nonprofit. We rented a house in Granada. It had a swimming pool in the living room. They all did. Every single one on Airbnb. So, we'd work hard on the barrio house in the morning and spend our afternoons lounging poolside and congratulating ourselves for a job well done. The hypocrisy strangled me. I pushed it to the side and tried not to dwell too much on it. My goal was to get my kids, thirteen, ten, and seven, through it. The hard work. The forty-five-minute walks in sweltering sunlight.

One morning we came to the site and in the ashes of their cooking fire was evidence of items we had brought from the States for the children. Burned edges of a Queen of Hearts nestled in the dust-packed yard where the family sat around heating up water for coffee. My oldest son raged.

"How could they do that? Those were gifts. They burned them in the fire?"

"You cannot judge. This isn't our life or our culture. You will never understand what their life is like."

I have always made it a strict rule when traveling not to judge that which I do not understand. I have also failed many times at this goal. But I do know I have never been truly, deeply hungry. I have never gone without clean water unless self-imposed while backpacking. I have never lived anything like this family. Maybe I would have done the same.

"You have to look at it from their point of view. They have no possessions. No shoes, no toys, no electricity, and barely any food. Maybe owning things is only important to us who have things to own."

"But it seems like if you don't have anything, you'd want to keep it nice when you got something," my son said.

"Or maybe the playing cards turned the fire blue. Or maybe he dropped them in anger. Maybe that's the lesson. We have too much. We own too much or put too much power into things. You cannot logically understand any of this. You can only take it with you and remember these moments when similar moments come back in your life. Like people you see at home who have seven dilapidated cars in their yard or broken fences, broken windows. Look at this life. They're living in dirt. That girl has a face infection. Maybe playing cards aren't really an issue. Maybe staying alive is."

You always wonder as a parent if anything gets through to your kid. Are they paying attention? Do they have enough experience to process what they're seeing? We don't get to find out until they're long gone and out of our house. I guess we can only hope.

In the end, the family didn't like the house. The mother's parting words were that it was *muy feo. Ugly.*

Our family walked home from the project on the last day, through streets with open sewers, and I just kept saying to myself and to my kids, "We cannot give up. We must keep trying."

Tolerance is the hardest human attribute I have ever attempted. But sometimes tolerance is merely validating another human being as worthy of your notice, your energy, your precious fifty-dollar-an-hour billable time. Perhaps we didn't better the life of the woman who got a new ugly house. Perhaps it was all just a learning lesson for my children instead.

{18}

Savvy

I screamed last night at nine thirty. Did you hear? It was pretty loud. My family was playing Legos in the living room, sifting through a mountain the size of a redwood stump, always sifting for that perfect piece. I yelled from the bathtub, "I won, I won! God dammit, I FUCKIN' WON."

"What did you win?" My husband is used to my dramatic outbursts. Despite the fact I was screaming, he kept sifting. I could see his face through the door, half smiling, half squinting at tiny plastic pieces. He needs glasses but won't admit it. He's always asking for more light.

"Karl! I won." Karl is my lender. Was my lender. A private lender, that is. They loan you money against a project you're working on at a super high interest rate in exchange for super efficient paperwork. You make handshake deals with them over coffee. They say stuff like, "So do we have a deal?" If you're picturing baseball bats and kneecaps, no, not like that.

Karl has always been kind to me. Trusted me. We've done a lot of deals together, and I've always been very business-like with him. He just wants his money, that's his job. So I've always paid him on time. Until last August. That's when the shit hit the fan, and a deal went bad. I couldn't get a loan to pay Karl back. I got denied for the first time. Ten weeks later, it happened again, then again. It was Sour Patch Kids all around. Really bad.

At first he was patient. The reason I got denied was partially his fault. The federal government didn't like his paperwork, so we were given a six-month "punishment." We had to wait. He was quiet during that time despite the fact he was in a perfect position to foreclose on my project. I stayed quiet, too, and started on yet another loan at the six-month mark.

Being a real estate investor in the post-2008 bubble is really frustrating. The rules put into place for people like me are so incredibly difficult to get through that it makes you wonder how people do it. The loan process for a bank is so involved that it can take up to six weeks just to gather all the correct paperwork. CPAs are asked for proof of their tax preparations; my property managers are asked for all leases to define washing machine responsibility; every property must be in very good working order. And the banks come back for more information for the entire duration of loan process, more proof you're only spending money on all the right stuff and none of the other stuff in life that pops up, like broken cars or kid's braces. The banks come dangerously close to asking you for a blood sample. My loans take almost fourteen weeks on average. For that many weeks, they scrutinize my insurance, my car, my write-offs, my kids' disabilities, everything.

Finally, a loan approval. One I deserved last summer. Time to get documents in place. They ask Karl for a payoff because the new bank loan is put into place just to pay him off. This will be the loan I keep on the project at a way lower interest rate for however long I own the property. I'll finally see a profit after two years. Karl sends over his payoff statement, and it's bloated beyond words. It's so high and filled with extras, I can't even read the number.

Karl decided to bleed me dry.

And that's when I decide to play the game using skills I probably inherited from my real Dad and learned to perfection by watching Mom hustle throughout my childhood. A lot of my business is a game. I used to tell people I'm a con artist, because quite frankly, I am. Bluffing to get the price you need to make a deal go through is the name of the game. Without a budget, you make no money. Without negotiation, every contractor would ask for the highest price. Without a profit, I cannot pay my own bills. So I negotiate and as soon as anybody negotiates, the con begins.

It's Friday at four when I receive the numbers from Karl. Friday at four is when I became a pro at this. I wrote him NO. Now part of the con is knowing what the other person needs. Karl needs his money, badly. He let it slip that he's trying to bankroll an apartment building for someone else. Bad info to give me. Now I know why he needs his money. I'd already agreed to pay him above and beyond his original loan, so I didn't feel bad about this part. But I sure as hell wasn't going to lose it all because he was angry. He'd let all those months slip by without getting testy, and he held it all in.

No, I won't pay it. He tells me he'll foreclose. Call in the note. I tell him, *Go for it.* I've got proof he accepted partial payment. Did I mention there were lawyers involved? Did I mention this went late into Friday night, all day Saturday, too? He texts back. *WE'LL foreclose on you. WE'LL sue you.*

I knew he just wanted his money back. He started getting personal. *You're a horrible person. You'll never make money again.*

Now here's a bit of advice for anyone who is non-confrontational. As soon as a non-personal argument turns personal, you've won. Guaranteed. You've got that guy by the balls. I say guy and balls because women are a different species. Far more complicated when it comes to confrontation. But I know the second a man says to me, "Now listen, I've been doing this for twenty-two years," or "You'll never make it, you fuckin' cunt," I've won. They're rattled and the rational side of the brain has just left the building.

Karl was rattled by late Saturday night when he texted to say he'd take my personal home as well. I read this while having cocktails with a friend in a classy bar. I smiled to myself, knowing it was working. *Okay*, I answered back. Here's another trick in negotiations. Say very little. It freaks people out.

Now you can feel sorry for Karl at this point. You should. He's a nice guy. He really is. Until he's not. But truly, deep down, he's a nice dad and husband. I've met his family. He mountain bikes with his son, surfs with his daughter. A nice guy. But first rule in business, it's not personal.

So when a guy calls me a cunt, threatens my livelihood, I don't take it personally. And yes, that happens. I'm a woman in a man's business. It's all they got, intimidation. I rarely lose my cool with them. I don't get personal either. That's what they want, to rattle me. You've got to have a game face.

Okay, take my house Karl. I'm too tired to care anymore.

Sunday morning, he started to lower the payoff number. That's when the Legos were brought out. By the time I was at Ikea buying new sheets for my kids' beds, Karl was texting me every half hour, *I'll call every lender in town, tell them you are a slacker.* I picked grey, orange, and blue sheets for the boys' beds. Casey's new favorite color is orange. He was gonna love it.

Hope you can find an apartment when the cops kick you out of your house. This, while I'm making dinner. Pasta with chicken and broccoli and a chocolate cake for Sunday night dessert. *Fine,* he writes, *I'll lower it $1,000 but you'd better sign tomorrow morning.* Cake was good.

While I'm reading Harry Potter to Casey, *Are you gonna sign in the morning?* Another, *Diana, answer my texts, ARE YOU GONNA SIGN?*

I started a bath, *NO.* Twenty minutes later while reading about the rebound of Buffalo, NY, an email comes from my title officer in charge of The Paperwork. "Karl dropped all the fees, you're good to go."

That's when you heard me yell. *I won.* And it felt delicious. Very delicious like that chocolate cake. I'm signing in an hour. A project I've worked on for three years and have yet to make a dime on. Not one single penny. Until today. Karl will be fine. He makes a year's profit the moment I sign. His ego got kicked though, and by a girl, too. A girl he once declared was Savvy with a capital S.

{19}

Apple Guy

I'm not a very noticeable person. I used to have great skin and tits, but time has done its damage. Now I'm just another person in line at Target, so I gather moments of flattery and savor them until maybe another one comes along. The other day, it was only a split second, but I caught it.

He was the guy at the Apple store. A Flock of Seagulls mixed with some Marilyn Manson on a Vespa. I immediately hated his condescending sneer when I told him I couldn't get my printer to scan onto my iPad. He smiled for a second, just enough to let me know what an idiot I was. Thirty minutes later, he still couldn't get it to work.

Meanwhile, I had to text and answer some phone calls for work. He asked about my job. "Sounds interesting," he said, not as condescending but definitely flavored. Next, he had to call the district manager to find an answer to my problem. A tech guy from the back room joined in the discussion on a three-way call. I sneered while emailing on a window bid.

A woman walked up to us and asked in Spanish if she could return her iPhone to this store. They told her they didn't speak Spanish, so I stepped in and translated. I asked her what country she was from. Guatemala. I told her how much I'd loved living in Antigua and that my family had built bicycle-powered wells for some farms nearby. She told me her family grew corn back home.

"Where did you learn Spanish?" he asked, seventeen layers into his iPad system.

"I haven't. I just travel a lot," I said.

Meanwhile, nothing got fixed. Nobody could solve my tech problem. Not the district manager, not the bench-techie, and not super important Apple guy. He told me, "We think your only choice is to get a MacBook."

"You mean *youuu* can't fix this? You, the Apple god guy, cannot make two systems have a conversation with one another? I'm appalled." Throwback of my head and big doe eyes. Added a very skillful wink. He smiled. A hipster smiled. Apparently, it happens. Then he checked out my tits. Fast and quick. An expert...except I saw.

When he looked back up at me, I threw him one of my single eyebrow lifts to let him know I saw. Experience gives you that cockiness to push boundaries beyond their current walls. His blush, stellar. Whole face blush. I hope his back broke out in a tiny sweat, too, pushing the boundaries on his crystal deodorant.

It was just a moment. A tiny one, but the older I get, the more I cling to them. I'm a flower in its over-bloomed stage, a rose with a few petals scattered below on the dirt. Strong, vibrant, colorful but not dewy anymore, not young and fresh and naive to how the world works. I am not noticed anymore. So I'll take what I can get while I still can. Even from a psuedo-Apple god—if need be.

{20}

No Thang

"No dates. None. You got that? No turning tricks when you're in my house."

I scrolled through dick pic after dick pic on my computer. I'd never before gone through the Men Seeking Men Craigslist ads until I needed to find Tom. It was more than shocking to find out they were all exactly the same. "Portland alpha male with ten inches seeking movies and/or ninja encounters." But none of them were Tom. He was simply gone.

When I met Tom in a Nicaraguan seaside resort, he said he'd noticed me the night before. He'd eavesdropped on a conversation I had with a young couple from Southern California. The conversation with the couple had not gone well. After spending two months in Nicaragua traveling backpacker style with my husband and three kids, I'd basically reached my peak tolerance for listening to early twenty-somethings in Central America teaching "sustainable farming practices" to the locals.

"Nicans can learn to eat healthier on a dollar a day."

"Um, yeah, except they make only four dollars day."

"They grow the majority of their foods in single crops."

"Yes, like we do in our country."

"But it can be done differently."

"So you're gonna save them from themselves? How good of you."

Tom had picked up how much I didn't like the couple and their Central American goals, a feeling he shared. The next morning, he asked to sit at my table over breakfast. He was good looking. Shaved tan head, light blue eyes, toned for middle age. We slowly eased into conversation that picked up speed.

We were aligned on all things regarding freedom—freedom of speech, body, motives, ideals. By afternoon, my sunburned husband looking drowsy from a nap, found me still sitting with Tom hashing out the world's problems one by one. After an hour and a couple of cold beers, the husband waved toward both of us, "You two are the same exact person." Besides the fact Tom was a British gay man, we were. And I knew it. It's rare I meet someone who can volley as fast as I can verbally and delve as deeply into the human psyche unashamed.

Two days later, I left to go home and Tom went back to England. We soon began writing regularly. I sent bitter unfiltered essays about the growing economic division regarding food pretentiousness. He would write late-night drunk stories of his sex life. How he left his former partner with a diagnosis of HIV, how he turned tricks for money, how he couch-surfed his way around Europe.

Early in the summer, Tom broke his dick working a job. I'm...not... kidding. Broke it at the perineum and almost had to have it removed.

He sent me photos from the hospital. It was black from the tip all the way up his crack. And Tom, being the world traveler with no address, also had no backup plan for an on-the-job injury. I said the only thing I could think of at the time, "Come here, I'll take care of you."

So Tom did. He flew to the States within days and stayed at one of our empty houses on the coast slated to be rehabbed the following summer. He loved it. Cleaned the craftsman windows, decorated the main floor with a green velvet couch from the thrift store and a quilt some grandma made. He nested for the first time in years. I'd stop by for a cider. He always kept a six-pack in the fridge, just for me.

The coastal town I'd recently moved my business to was a much smaller community than I'd ever worked in before. Good ol' boy society still alive, and although the hipsters were arriving with their bikes daily, the ingrained fishing industry is conservative. I worried a little about Tom's safety. When we went to bars together, I made no jokes, no sexual innuendos, and neither did he. We spoke through our eyes and I could read his mind. I reminded him he was still healing.

"That's fine, luv, my cock is broke. No Grindr for me."

Some of my employees would come from Portland to work on the coast. They'd stay at Tom's house, each room outfitted with a bed and end table. I set it up like a hotel for just this reason. And Tom was a great host. He'd make bagel sandwiches for everyone before work, stock the fridge with beer, and nobody was the wiser. Nobody knew why or what Tom had going on in his life.

Especially Aaron, who does my tile work and also stays in Portland at another of our places. He's a sweet, naive, hot-as-shit Minnesota boy, and on more than a few occasions, the two of them cruised town "searching for pussy." Which made Tom and me giggle afterward. He never seemed to care if he had to cover up a little of his life. His job had taught him to be a good actor. Something the con artist in me could relate to.

At this point, I'd been working with all men for years. Hardened men who work with their hands in bad weather. They drank hard, worked their bodies to the breaking point and sometimes, simply didn't have the head space to learn about life's evolving moral codes. Such as misogyny or flagrant homophobia. I'd learned, like Tom, to change accordingly, when necessary. I picked my battles and knew when to keep my mouth shut. Tom and I both seemed to get this. We had a lot of fun smoking weed by the water and talking about our chameleon abilities.

Like all friendships, our honeymoon began to fade. I caught Tom lying to me about his Grindr profile; then he told me he was gonna start making money again, his way. Regardless of our deal. He'd already asked Aaron if he could stay with him in Portland on the weekends.

"Look, luv, Portland is a cock and ball gold mine. A few fists and trolls, maybe a video or two, and I'll be all set up for a winter in Mexico. I just need you to front me a MacBook and an iPhone."

In zero to sixty, I lost my shit.

Lost it.

"You're going to stay with my employee and a tenant in my apartment building and fuck guys, what, on Aaron's couch? He thinks you're hetero, asshole. You don't think that's gonna freak him out after your little pussy patrol game? No, no fucking way am I helping you!"

The texts started at four after I'd left him standing in his living room.

I'd never gotten mad at Tom before. He was shocked at my emotion. I was shocked at his shock. We'd had a deal.

I'm disappointed in you, luv. I thought you were different than all the rest.

I am. I thought you'd keep your promise. No tricks in my houses.

Don't let your ego smack you on the way to the bank, sweetheart.

My trips to the bank have funded two months of your recovery. You're welcome, prick.

The last thing I wanted was my HIV-positive, broken-dicked British friend getting busted while on U.S. soil, under my roof, with one of my employees. I had visions of his face broken in a hospital room or meeting with lawyers to get him his HIV meds from England. I'd already reached my max responsibility levels years ago, after my third kid was born. I really couldn't do more if Tom made one mistake. I was hanging on by a thread.

Your cunt keeps flapping but all I hear is an 80 IQ.

Finally, after hours and hours of texts to and from Tom, who eventually stopped responding, I sent my husband over the next morning to make sure he was okay. Tom had stayed up the previous night drinking, crying, losing his shit.

Tom, you need to sleep this off. We'll talk in person after you fucking sleep. Sober up dude. We can talk later.

I worried he'd do something stupid, like burn the house down or try to pick up a guy at one of the local bars. By the time Steve got there, Tom was pacing around caged, exhausted, determined to have the final word. He had packed up his stuff.

I found one of his friends on Facebook and contacted her. "Please call Tom, he's losing his shit." She wrote back, "He's a stubborn bastard, it won't work." And it didn't. Steve gave him some cash, and Tom disappeared. Blocked from Facebook and all lines of communication. Gone. Tom was out there. Probably somewhere in Portland without enough money to get back to England.

Which is how I ended up on Craigslist. Maybe I could recognize his dick or his writing style, I thought. I'd seen his ads in England. He'd sent them to me early on in our relationship. He'd say he was ten years younger than he was. That his dick was bigger than it was. And he never once mentioned his HIV status.

Last week, I did something I've never done. I went to the Other box in my Facebook messages. And there it was. A message from Tom, months old. A well-written swirling bit of anger and pain in 500 words telling me I was the most horrible piece of shit that ever walked the earth, that I was garbage and deserved to be gang-raped throughout eternity. And he got his final word.

It ended with, "You are NO THANG."

{21}

Mom Boobs

They'd drag their tranquilized zombie legs from room to room and try to dance to techno beats thumping around decorations of toilets filled with blinking lights under plastic ice, all in the name of "art."

Isaac and Patty were my brand new BFFs I had met twelve hours before at the nouveau Detroit Hostel. We had bonded hard that afternoon, first at an Irish pub called Nancy's Whiskey, then at a lager house that played punk. I was still riding a high after a man with devil horns imbedded in his bald head bought me a shot of tequila and threw me a wink.

But my new BFF's peer pressure to hit an after-party was simply adorable.

"We'll keep an eye on you. Don't worry. I have an Uber app."

"You guys can't leave me alone. I'll never find you in a giant party."

"It'll be cool."

The city seemed like a burned-up forest, and I was just a deer walking through a charred meadow. It should have scared me. An after-party in a warehouse somewhere in Detroit is not where most people my age would be. But I felt invigorated in this city that had few cops or street signs. A Wild West with pavement. A playground for hustlers.

Honestly, I was eight vodka tonics into a night that felt a lot like riding a bike with freshly shaved legs and no idea what an Uber app even was.

Our driver to the party was Bin, a friend of Isaac's he'd met through people who knew people. At one in the morning, Bin suggested we stop for more alcohol. I was thinking, I sure as hell didn't need more but along I went. To a liquor store somewhere, in the middle of somewhere. I texted my husband back home in Portland.

I'm heading to an after-party with two people from the hostel and a guy named Bin. I've got my phone, a credit card, my ID, and some cash. As if this was going to save me on a dark street corner.

We pulled up in our Chevy or some kinda car Bin drove that reminded me of the suburbs. There were black SUVs parked in front of a blinking *Liquor* sign in neon. Their drivers leaned against the graffitied brick wall and winked at Patty before saying, "What's up Tokyo?" while she giggled and ran inside to buy some Donettes and MGD. I mentally noted, "Uhm, they're packing heat inside those back belts."

Have fun and be safe, lit up my phone screen while we climbed back into our overloaded car, heavy with twelve packs, ready for takeoff.

Bin drove us through blacked-out avenues that hadn't seen a streetlight in at least ten years to the warehouse gallery while Isaac in the backseat promised again not to ditch me once we got inside. Bin said he'd keep an eye on me, too, and Patty reminded me she had that Uber app. I began to feel like I was a circus clown they were bringing to a birthday party.

"Hey, look, we brought a mom in clogs in case anyone thinks they might puke."

I waited for the insecurities to pop up, the Goodyear blimp to play across my brain screen.

YOU AREN'T THIS PERSON ANYMORE. YOU'RE OLD.

But it didn't. I was caught up in spring fever. A young colt kicking my legs in the warm air. I was free from caring about whatever these twenty-somethings could throw my way. I didn't need to be skinny or attractive or funny or the best dancer tonight. I was forty-five. Nobody was gonna notice me and my Mom boobs. Not in this crowd. I wasn't trying to be anything but me.

Within seconds it became so familiar, a different decade. At the door, the guy collecting cash had an attitude that made me chuckle. For a night, he was a god. He reminded me of Andrew Dice Clay with the thick sideburns—sitting on a stool telling jokes as he took money, high-fiving and fist-bumping acquaintances, pinching buds out from his jar full of weed for all his friends. The in-crowd.

Once inside, Isaac began his search for his one-night stand, Patty began dancing with a mirror, and Bin handed out bags of weed from his JanSport backpack. If Depeche Mode had started playing, I would have asked Bin if he had slipped me a tab. It felt like 1987 all over again, but now I had no little bottle of Rush in my pocket, no Madonna rag tied in my hair. Nope, now I was wearing a bra with an underwire and comfortable shoes.

I headed for the bathroom before they got trashed. Bin knew of a secret location behind a kicked-out wall. I squeezed between two-by-fours and broken sheetrock to find a second boy's bathroom. Bin stood guard outside which made us instant BFFs. The lights inside were fluorescent and ridiculously bright. There was a plastic orange chair in the corner, the kind we had in elementary school with a hole in the back. This one had a white guy with a short mohawk shooting up into his arm, dangling on the only sink. Both of our faces reflected sickly in the giant utility mirror. I peed as fast as I could into a urine-stained bowl and never flushed, then washed my hands near his arm and smiled while his eyes began to roll back. I ducked out quickly, not wanting the seedy scene to infect my current adrenaline high.

Not wanting to think.

The hallway from the bathroom was lined with benches and there sat the most fucked-up of the fucked-ups who couldn't stand anymore. The passed-out drunk girl with the flower skirt and painted nails. The sweaty overweight guy wondering if he's gonna puke but still yelling at girls passing by like he might get lucky. And those zombies dragging their legs around and not able to hold their arms up. Mental note: *Ask Isaac what's up with the zombies.*

And next to me, a guy named Cory.

"Hey, how's it going?" His eyes were clear, and he seemed to be able to retain the use of his jaw properly. In a building with more coke than Coke in Georgia, it was impressive to see somebody not chewing off their bottom lip, able to talk.

"Good, how about you?" He smiled with beautiful teeth under a freckled nose. Very Ohio corn-country, dressed up in jeans and a yellow rain slicker.

It wasn't raining.

"You need anything tonight?" he asked while his eyes met all who passed by, looking for something better.

I kept thinking about how much I wanted a Denver omelet and hash browns, but I'm not sure everybody knows what a Denver omelet is. I'm not sure Cory would get my humor. "No, no, I'm good. Thanks."

"All right, if you need anything, just ask. I've got it all." He emphasized the all like it was a dirty menu. "I'm Cory. Just ask around for Cory."

Curiosity got me, and I wasn't letting him go until I figured out what it all was. "Like what? Share. I wanna know whatcha got."

"I've got Ks and Cs, Blues, taps, friendlies, and I think I've even got some oysters."

What the fuck is an oyster?

"Okay, I don't want any of that, but could you please tell me what all of that is because I find it kinda fascinating."

His eyes darted through the crowd but a smile crawled up that nubile cheek. He wouldn't really look at me. He was busy scanning the swaying room of dancers and zombies. Checking the pulse buzzing with probably 200 people jumping and laughing, blood pumping through their veins thick with oysters and dots and what did he say, Ks?

"Tell me, what's a K?"

"How about this, I'll tell you what a K is if you take one?"

"Ha!" Yep, that's a hilarious notion. I'm gonna take an unidentified pill from a guy wearing a questionable yellow rain slicker on a clear-sky evening. Even in my heyday, I never swallowed pills. I just didn't like them. I had no problem smoking anything people gave me and that proved to be a poor choice here and there but tonight, no. I'd had my limit of being a badass mutha.

"I don't think so. Not tonight—"

"Well, you're missing out." He stood up with those final words and walked toward the DJs perched behind a shower installation that two girls were dancing inside. They were probably six feet tall with their afros, leggy models wearing sunglasses to fight off the strobelight mounted to the shower head. Nouveau Detroit was all here. Business-minded artists trying to create their own brain melts and ride into better days.

In the twenty years since I walked away from a dancing, drug-fueled nightlife, there have been times that I've missed this feeling. Usually during those long weeks of repetitive motion. Dinners and hundreds of "Mom, what's behind a black hole?" and "What happens if you puke in zero gravity?" I've romanticized this feeling of freedom. Romanticized in a way that is true in a lot of ways. Sitting in that warehouse right then, I was invisible. Free to walk, talk, or get inside that shower installation with those women and dance my ass off. I felt glad for the choice. And the experience. But it was time to get the fuck outta here.

Time to find Patti. Time to figure out what the hell an Uber app was and get my fat ass home. It was four in the morning, and I was beginning to sober up and feel hung over. I didn't feel like seeing the zombies sober. My bed at the hostel was tolerably comfortable, and this night had already been fun enough to sustain me through the endless conversations moms have about homemade window cleaners for twenty-two minutes too long. Next time, I'd just sit during that Mama clutch discussion and remember Cory's little K pill and giggle to myself because I once spent a night in big bad Detroit with a drug dealer. Cuz I'm all gangsta—with Mom boobs.

{22}

Crush

I sometimes crush on people. Like a friendship crush. Ya know what I mean? You meet someone at a party or maybe even online, and you just kinda know you'd be good together. Like chemistry good. You want to be friends. You want to do lunch or share jokes, maybe even laugh about guys at the Apple store, but there always seems to be something in the way.

My friend Annie and I met that way years ago. I'm not even sure where it started but because of mutual friends, we'd chat at various social gigs, and I just knew we could last longer than polite conversation. But like a movie, roadblocks flew up along the way. She'd just had a baby, there were other friends who felt territorial over us. It was difficult to bridge into the BFF part. We needed that first date without the others distracting us. I finally "asked" her out. It was awkward. I mean, so much of early friendship is just dating without sex, right?

Writer Liz Prato once wrote that she'd found the secret Facebook page that showed all the people who had decided not to grant her friendship request. She'd written, "Why? I'm a good person."

I laughed because it's true, right? Why do people not want to be your friend? Is it your profile photo on social media? Is it because you say fuck a lot in person? Are you too sarcastic the one time they met you? Or not pretty enough, or cool enough or witty enough...that night? What if you might be the best person they've ever spent time with but you just never got the chance to show them because you were wearing turquoise and they loathe turquoise?

My friend Jennifer and I share a mysterious faceless Facebook friend who maintains alias status. He intrigues us, and we've decided that he must be so incredibly good-looking, that to show his hideous face online would burn our corneas. That's what we joke about. The truth is, we don't know why he's anonymous. But we both kinda crush. We love his weird posts: "The synesthesia when the sight of male anatomy gives you a shot of lost cigarettes." What? Perhaps he's a genius. Or just weird enough for her and I to tangle brain matters with occasionally. Kinda like a video game for adults. Or perhaps he's just a normal dude or dudette who enjoys the freedom of anonymity. Either way, we both feel a kindred spirit with this elusive person based on nothing but a few words here and there. We can tell we'd click somehow if real life didn't get so complicated with outward perceptions and sexual overtones.

When I'm in these situations, where I want to be friends with someone, when I want to take it to the next level past business casual or "Nice to meet yas," is exactly when every single movie from my childhood comes into play. Every boy crush I've ever had. I get nervous, I act stupid or ridiculous, and I usually burn all chances to become friends. I over-reach. I over-try. I sit with spinach in my teeth, a booger in my nose; I act like a court jester. Nothing can go right, and I slink away ashamed that I just couldn't pull off the Jennifer Lawrence.

And it goes both ways, right? It's hard when you become disillusioned, after the newness wears off. When you realize what you thought was a witty dry sense of humor is actually just a bitter broken human across the lunch table. Or that funny way they talk, that was so charming at first, is just a shy version of armor. Unbreakable armor. And the early excitement of a new friendship begins to fade.

I recently watched a group of respectable women speak about feminism. I was excited about the discussion after reading the work these women had put forth into the world. Initially, my heart was beating fast in anticipation of being surrounded by like-minded "womyn." New future friends, perhaps?

But once the illusion cracked open and words spilled forth, I realized that despite our shared ages and gender, we were on much different pages. One woman said, "We need to be nicer and kinder to our women friends." I thought, "No! We need to get real. Stop pretending like life is filled with beach yoga poses and gratitude-filled sunsets. Sometimes life sucks, people! Amirite? Sometimes women are bitches. Sometimes I'm a bitch!" I had convinced myself we would all be in a BJ Club together and laugh merrily with vodka, but instead they wanted hugs. I wouldn't belong, again.

I disappoint my own crushes. I know I do. When someone meets me and is attracted to my hearty laugh, my wit, and my flirt, they assume I will entertain them at all times, and we shall be one. But I am also an intense thinker who over-probes and over-examines human emotions to the point that my new crush may eventually feel uncomfortable and walk away feeling a bit violated from my honesty. And the cycle continues as we just bump around together sharing our stories, gathering knowledge and hopefully some grace as we go. Trying to find our match—another human who can understand our rants, our pleasures, our intentions. Who can forgive us when we're selfish, forget when we are brutal and remember when we try.

And maybe, if the stars align and a round peg miraculously fits into a square hole, and I can relax and let go, and you can relax and let go, and we end up at lunch, laughing and talking about Vikings, hand jobs, and hippies, then we shall crush, dammit! Over sushi and jelly doughnuts. And it will be good.

See more of Diana Kirk's work

dianakirk.wordpress.com

{Acknowledgments}

When I look at how I got here, to this very spot, with you holding my first book in your hands, I can honestly say four humans made it happen.

First and foremost, Mom. The woman who taught me how to read and write before kindergarten. Who encouraged me to speak up. Reminded me I wasn't the only one who thought the words going through my head. Who showed me how to work hard to get what I wanted in life. I only stand tall because I'm standing on her shoulders.

My BFF Rachel Allen. Nobody on this spinning orb has spent as much time as this woman, for the last twenty-five years, listening to my stories on loop. She was always there when it felt as if my arms would give out from swimming against currents. Her loyalty and friendship have meant as much as my marriage at times. And I'm fairly sure she's saved my life.

Author Ariel Gore was the first person who ever planted a seed in my brain that maybe, just maybe, I should continue writing my stories past my weekend hobby. She said, "You got this" when I really needed to hear it and then said "publish" when I was ready. She is the very description of a writing mentor who knows when to give that little push.

Author and publisher at Black Bomb Books, Jennifer Fulford, wrote me on Facebook one day and said, "You're an essayist with an edge. I have an idea." Now you're holding her idea.

I also pay homage to many writer pals, including Wayward Writers like Kitty Torres or Tara Lynn Marcelle, who stepped up and sent me notes, "You're doing great, keep going." When Bonnie Divitelsen invited me to read for her Penduline Press series. When Jodie Fleming asked me to write on her *The Psychology of It* website. When Ayun Halliday said, "No story tells the whole story." When fellow author Jennifer Robin reminded me I'm only human. When Gigi Duncan and Suze Pierce spent their free time reading my stories, offering guidance and advice. When photographer Anna Yarrow took my photos and made me giggle, and Yanay Tsabary reminded me not to apologize. And when Deirdre Nagle said, "You crack me up," and I answered, "Let's drink, bitch!"

Not enough could be said about my team called family, Ryder, Phelan, and Casey and their beautiful daddy Steve. My in-laws who inspire, my parents who support, and my ever insightful cousin, Shannon Copstead, who said to me one summer day, "You've done a lot with your life. I think you should write about it." Everyone, I thank you. You are my gooey center. I am but a shell without all of you. ~ *Diana Kirk, Summer 2016*

{Epilogue}

I was in Trader Joe's today checking out, making small talk with the guy at the register. I mentioned I was writing a story in my head while shopping and ended up buying weird stuff that I never do based solely on the product descriptions.

He says, "Oh, so you're a writer?"

I laughed. No, no, I shake my head. "I'm taking a writing class right now and trying to come up with an idea for this week's assignment."

So he says, "Oh, so you're a writer?"

At this point, I giggle because obviously he's a writer, too, and understands how hard it is to say you're a writer when really you run a company and talk budgets and deadlines all day.

"Okay, you got me. I write, yes. I even got my first short story published recently. But it's just a short story."

Then the woman behind me, who's eavesdropping, leans over and touches my shoulder, "Congrats, that's so awesome."

Now I'm totally embarrassed because other people are looking over at me and then the checkout guy pulls out a piece of paper from his pocket and asks, "What's your name so I can look you up?"

Another lady in line says, "Yeah, what's your name, do you have a book?" Now my hand is at my mouth chewing on a fingernail and I'm like, "Seriously, it's just a breast cancer story I made up, kinda silly."

I'm literally trying to fold myself up into my purse when the woman says, "I'm a breast cancer survivor," and I'm purple now and feeling like this is never gonna end, and then the checkout guy RINGS THE DAMN BELL! HE RINGS THE DAMN TRADER JOE'S BELL, and yells out, "She's a published author!"

People clap, and my eyes are six inches wide, and my jaw is on the floor. "I cannot believe you just did that."

He chuckles and then says, "There's your Trader Joe's story."

Made in the USA
Middletown, DE
05 September 2019